THE KINGFISHER
ATLAS OF
EXPLORATION
&EMPIRES

Simon Adams
Illustrated by Mark Bergin

KINGFISHER

KINGFISHER

Kingfisher Publications Plc
New Penderel House
283–288 High Holborn
London WC1V 7HZ
www.kingfisherpub.com

Senior editor: Simon Holland
Designers: Ray Bryant, Heidi Appleton, Jack Clucas, Mike Davis
Cover designers: Jack Clucas, Malcolm Parchment
Consultant: Professor Jeremy Black, University of Exeter
Picture research manager: Cee Weston-Baker
Senior production controller: Jessamy Oldfield
DTP co-ordinator: Catherine Hibbert
Indexer: Catherine Brereton

Cartography by: Colin and Ian McCarthy
              Maidenhead Cartographic Services Limited,
              Maidenhead, Berkshire

First published by Kingfisher Publications Plc 2007
10 9 8 7 6 5 4 3 2 1

1TR/0207/SHENS/SCHOY(SCHOY)/128MA/C

ISBN: 978 0 7534 1374 6

Copyright © Kingfisher Publications Plc 2007

A CIP record for this book is available from the British Library.

Printed in Taiwan

CONTENTS

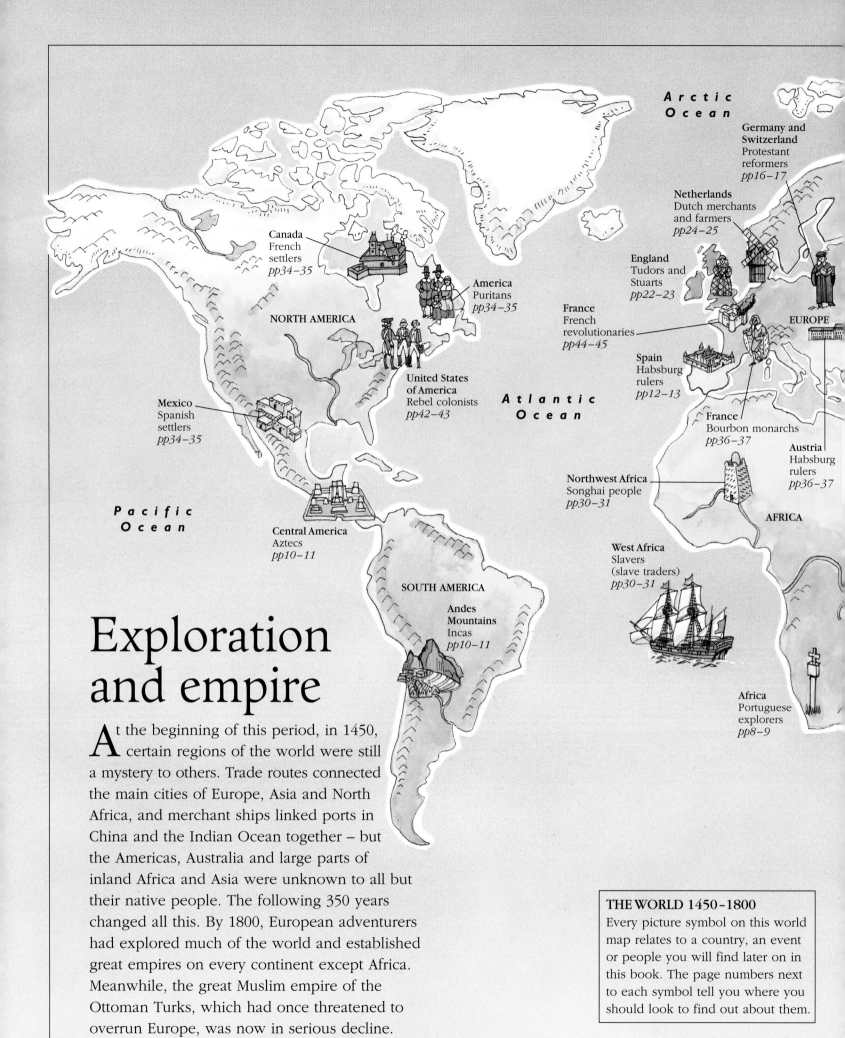

Canada
French
settlers
pp34–35

America
Puritans
pp34–35

NORTH AMERICA

United States
of America
Rebel colonists
pp42–43

Mexico
Spanish
settlers
pp34–35

Central America
Aztecs
pp10–11

SOUTH AMERICA

Andes
Mountains
Incas
pp10–11

*Arctic
Ocean*

Germany and
Switzerland
Protestant
reformers
pp16–17

Netherlands
Dutch merchants
and farmers
pp24–25

England
Tudors and
Stuarts
pp22–23

France
French
revolutionaries
pp44–45

EUROPE

Spain
Habsburg
rulers
pp12–13

France
Bourbon monarchs
pp36–37

Austria
Habsburg
rulers
pp36–37

*Atlantic
Ocean*

Northwest Africa
Songhai people
pp30–31

AFRICA

West Africa
Slavers
(slave traders)
pp30–31

*Pacific
Ocean*

Africa
Portuguese
explorers
pp8–9

Exploration and empire

At the beginning of this period, in 1450, certain regions of the world were still a mystery to others. Trade routes connected the main cities of Europe, Asia and North Africa, and merchant ships linked ports in China and the Indian Ocean together – but the Americas, Australia and large parts of inland Africa and Asia were unknown to all but their native people. The following 350 years changed all this. By 1800, European adventurers had explored much of the world and established great empires on every continent except Africa. Meanwhile, the great Muslim empire of the Ottoman Turks, which had once threatened to overrun Europe, was now in serious decline.

THE WORLD 1450–1800
Every picture symbol on this world map relates to a country, an event or people you will find later on in this book. The page numbers next to each symbol tell you where you should look to find out about them.

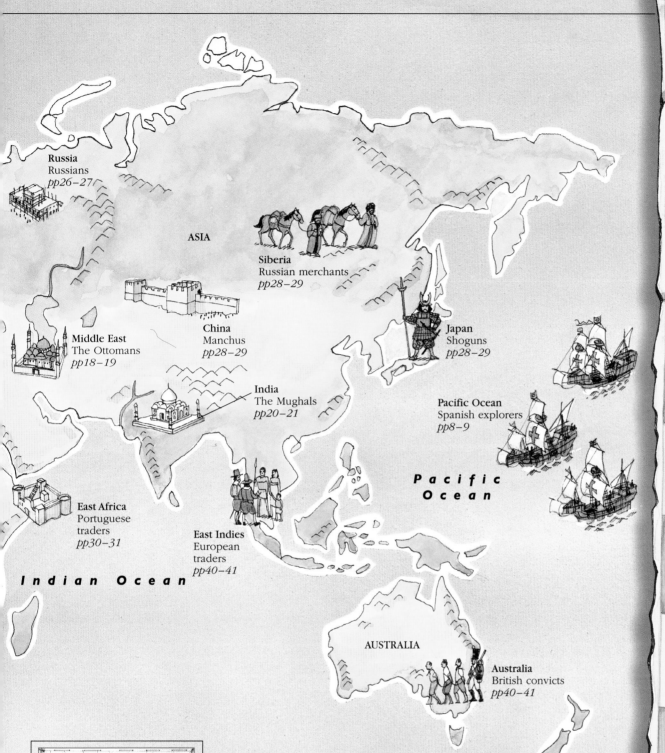

Russia
Russians
pp26–27

ASIA

Siberia
Russian merchants
pp28–29

China
Manchus
pp28–29

Japan
Shoguns
pp28–29

Middle East
The Ottomans
pp18–19

India
The Mughals
pp20–21

Pacific Ocean
Spanish explorers
pp8–9

*Pacific
Ocean*

East Africa
Portuguese
traders
pp30–31

East Indies
European
traders
pp40–41

Indian Ocean

AUSTRALIA

Australia
British convicts
pp40–41

LOCATOR MAP

You will find a world map
like this along with every
map in the book. This
allows you to see exactly
which part of the world the
main map is showing you.

KEY TO MAPS IN THIS BOOK

JAPAN	Main region or country
Deccan	Other region or province
■ PARIS	Capital city
● Yorktown	City, town or village
Zambezi	River, lake or island
Andes	Ocean, sea, desert or mountain range
– – –	National boundary
- - - - -	Empire boundary

1400

1450 Renaissance cultural movement
flourishes in western Europe
1453 Ottomans capture Constantinople,
bringing the ancient Byzantine
empire to an end

1479 Ferdinand of Aragon and Isabella
of Castile join their thrones through
marriage to unite Spain
1480 Muscovy becomes
an independent state
1485 Tudor dynasty begins
to rule England
1492 Christopher Columbus
first lands in the New World
1498 Vasco da Gama becomes
the first European to sail
around Africa to Asia

1500

1510 Portuguese found Goa,
first European colony in Asia
1517 Martin Luther begins the
Protestant Reformation in Europe
1517 Regular shipment of African
slaves to the Americas begins
1519 Charles V of Spain is Holy Roman
Emperor; Habsburgs dominate Europe
1519–22 Magellan and crew complete
the first circumnavigation of the world
1519–33 Spanish capture
Aztec and Inca empires
1526 Mughals invade India
1534 Jacques Cartier explores Canada
1543 Copernicus proposes that the Sun
is at the centre of the solar system
1545 Catholic Counter-Reformation begins
1556 Charles V divides vast Habsburg
empire between Spain and Austria
1558–1603 Elizabeth I rules England
1568 Dutch rebel against Spanish rule

1600

1603 England and Scottish crowns
united under King James I
1603 Tokugawa shoguns rule Japan
1607 English establish their first
permanent colony in North America
1608 French begin to colonize Canada
1618–48 Thirty Years' War engulfs Europe

1643–1715 Louis XIV rules France
1644 Ming dynasty begins in China
1648 Dutch win official
independence from Spain
1649–60 Britain becomes a republic after
civil war leads to the execution of its king
1667 Dutch control the Spice Islands
1682–1725 Peter the
Great modernizes Russia
1683 Ottomans fail to capture Vienna
as their empire begins to decline
1698 Portuguese expelled
from the east African coast

1700

1700 Enlightenment cultural
movement flourishes in Europe
1707 Mughal empire at its height

1740 Maria Theresa builds the
powerful Austrian empire
1740–86 Frederick the Great builds
up Prussian military power

1763 British drive the French
out of North America
1770 Captain Cook lands in Australia
1775–81 American revolutionary war
1776 Thirteen British colonies in
America declare their independence
1789 George Washington
becomes first US president
1789 Revolution breaks out in France
1799 Napoleon Bonaparte
takes power in France

1800

The world 1450–1800:
What we know about the past

The world changed rapidly after 1450. Inventions long known to the Chinese, such as printing and gunpowder, transformed the world when Europeans discovered them for themselves and then exported them to other continents. New ship designs and navigational aids helped European adventurers to explore and then conquer much of the globe. In some countries, systems of government based on the rule of an emperor or king were gradually replaced with 'democratic' rule by the people, although democracy of this kind would not be widespread until the late 19th century. Not everyone was affected at the same time or same speed by these changes, but the world of 1800 was very different to the world of 1450.

Printing
In a German town called Mainz, in 1448, Johann Gutenberg developed a printing press that used movable type. This led to a revolution in learning, as more and more people were able to obtain and read printed books and pamphlets on a wide range of subjects. It also allowed new or revolutionary ideas to circulate freely as never before. Gutenberg's first printed book was the Bible (above).

Democracy
The intellectual revolution of the 18th century – known as the Enlightenment – led many people to question how they were governed, and to seek to govern themselves through a democracy. By 1800, democratically elected parliaments ruled some western European nations, as well as the United States of America. The picture above shows America's Declaration of Independence from British rule, which took place in 1776.

Powerful monarchs
After 1640, a series of powerful kings ruled in Europe. They were known as 'absolute monarchs' because they believed that they held total power and were answerable to nobody else on Earth. One of the most powerful of these kings was Frederick the Great of Prussia (ruled 1740–86), who ordered the construction of the Neue Palais (below) at Potsdam, outside Berlin in Germany.

The Neue Palais was built in 1763–69 to celebrate Prussia's successes in the Seven Years' War (1756–63) against Austria, France and Russia.

Palace contains more than 200 rooms, including four state reception rooms

New forms of warfare

Gunpowder was known to the Chinese and possibly the Arabs by the 10th century, but its use in Europe from the 14th century onwards revolutionized warfare. European armies used gunpowder to fire lead bullets from rifles and muskets. Armed with these weapons, they easily overwhelmed their opponents, helping them to conquer large parts of the globe by 1800.

Early 17th-century European wheel-lock pistol

Exploration

European navigators began to explore the rest of the world after 1450, discovering the American continent and a new sea route to Asia around the south of Africa. These voyages allowed Europeans to dominate world trade and to set up colonies in every continent. In this picture, Dutch merchants are trading with native Americans in what is now New York.

More than 400 sandstone statues, mass-produced by a team of sculptors

Southern wing contains Frederick's apartments and a small theatre used for operas

Statues of the Three Graces (Beauty, Mirth and Good Cheer) support the Prussian royal crown

Voyages of discovery

In the mid-1400s, European sailors explored the oceans in search of trade, wealth and conquest. The Portuguese led the way, exploring the coast of Africa and discovering a sea route to India and Asia. The Spanish sponsored (financially supported) Columbus to find a westerly sea route to Asia. Instead he found America. The English and French then looked for a northwest route to Asia around the north of North America, while the Dutch looked for a northeast route around Siberia. By 1600, Europeans ruled the seas.

See inset (below)

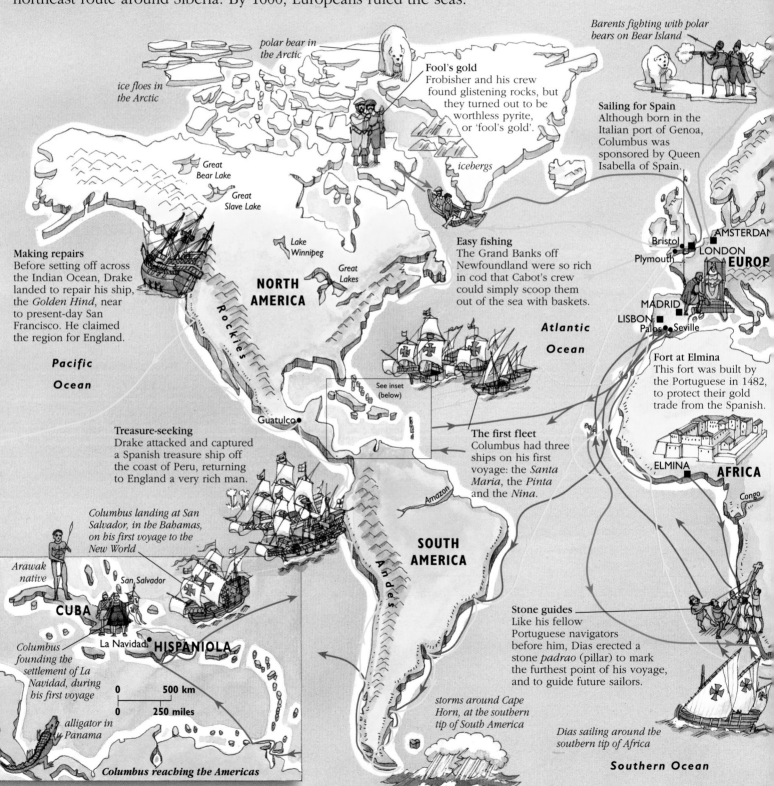

KEY TO VOYAGES

Bartolomeu Dias	1487–88
Christopher Columbus: 1st voyage	1492–93
John Cabot	1497
Vasco da Gama	1497–98
Christopher Columbus: 3rd voyage	1498–1500
Ferdinand Magellan & Sebastián de Elcano	1519–22
Martin Frobisher	1576
Francis Drake	1577–80
Willem Barents	1596–98

Arctic Ocean

Barents fighting with polar bears on Bear Island

polar bear in the Arctic

Fool's gold
Frobisher and his crew found glistening rocks, but they turned out to be worthless pyrite, or 'fool's gold'.

ice floes in the Arctic

icebergs

Sailing for Spain
Although born in the Italian port of Genoa, Columbus was sponsored by Queen Isabella of Spain.

Great Bear Lake

Great Slave Lake

Lake Winnipeg

Great Lakes

NORTH AMERICA

Rockies

Making repairs
Before setting off across the Indian Ocean, Drake landed to repair his ship, the *Golden Hind*, near to present-day San Francisco. He claimed the region for England.

Pacific Ocean

Easy fishing
The Grand Banks off Newfoundland were so rich in cod that Cabot's crew could simply scoop them out of the sea with baskets.

AMSTERDAM
Bristol
LONDON
Plymouth
EUROPE

MADRID
LISBON
Palos Seville

Atlantic Ocean

Fort at Elmina
This fort was built by the Portuguese in 1482, to protect their gold trade from the Spanish.

ELMINA

AFRICA

Congo

The first fleet
Columbus had three ships on his first voyage: the *Santa Maria*, the *Pinta* and the *Nina*.

Guatulco

Treasure-seeking
Drake attacked and captured a Spanish treasure ship off the coast of Peru, returning to England a very rich man.

Columbus landing at San Salvador, in the Bahamas, on his first voyage to the New World

Amazon

Andes

SOUTH AMERICA

Stone guides
Like his fellow Portuguese navigators before him, Dias erected a stone *padrao* (pillar) to mark the furthest point of his voyage, and to guide future sailors.

storms around Cape Horn, at the southern tip of South America

Dias sailing around the southern tip of Africa

Southern Ocean

Arawak native

San Salvador

CUBA

Columbus founding the settlement of La Navidad, during his first voyage

La Navidad **HISPANIOLA**

0	500 km
0	250 miles

alligator in Panama

Columbus reaching the Americas

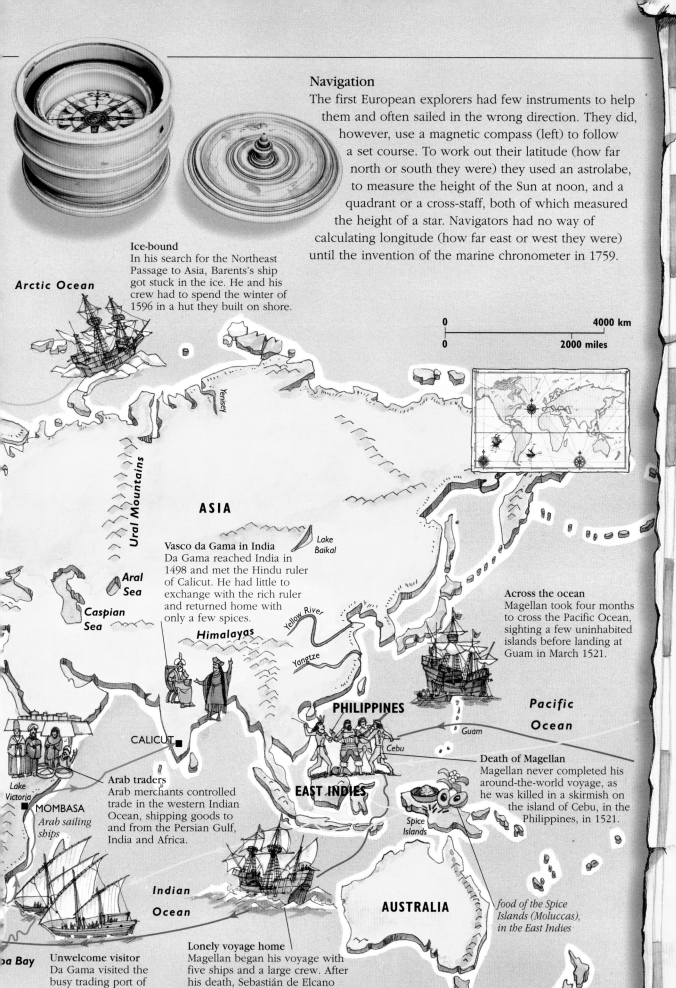

Navigation

The first European explorers had few instruments to help them and often sailed in the wrong direction. They did, however, use a magnetic compass (left) to follow a set course. To work out their latitude (how far north or south they were) they used an astrolabe, to measure the height of the Sun at noon, and a quadrant or a cross-staff, both of which measured the height of a star. Navigators had no way of calculating longitude (how far east or west they were) until the invention of the marine chronometer in 1759.

Ice-bound
In his search for the Northeast Passage to Asia, Barents's ship got stuck in the ice. He and his crew had to spend the winter of 1596 in a hut they built on shore.

Arctic Ocean

0 ———————— 4000 km
0 ———————— 2000 miles

ASIA

Ural Mountains

Yenisey

Lake Baikal

Vasco da Gama in India
Da Gama reached India in 1498 and met the Hindu ruler of Calicut. He had little to exchange with the rich ruler and returned home with only a few spices.

Aral Sea

Caspian Sea

Himalayas

Yellow River

Yangtze

Across the ocean
Magellan took four months to cross the Pacific Ocean, sighting a few uninhabited islands before landing at Guam in March 1521.

PHILIPPINES

Pacific Ocean

Guam

Cebu

CALICUT ■

Arab traders
Arab merchants controlled trade in the western Indian Ocean, shipping goods to and from the Persian Gulf, India and Africa.

Death of Magellan
Magellan never completed his around-the-world voyage, as he was killed in a skirmish on the island of Cebu, in the Philippines, in 1521.

Lake Victoria

■ **MOMBASA**
Arab sailing ships

EAST INDIES

Spice Islands

Indian Ocean

AUSTRALIA

food of the Spice Islands (Moluccas), in the East Indies

a Bay

Unwelcome visitor
Da Gama visited the busy trading port of Mombasa, but fled when the local Muslim ruler attacked his two ships.

Lonely voyage home
Magellan began his voyage with five ships and a large crew. After his death, Sebastián de Elcano battled through storms to return home to Spain in 1522, with only one ship and 17 other men.

Southern Ocean

1450–1600

1450

1460 Death of Prince Henry 'the Navigator', the first Portuguese sponsor (financial supporter) of voyages of discovery

1485–86 Diogo Cao sails down the length of the west African coast for Portugal

1487–88 Dias becomes first European to sail around the southern tip of Africa into the Indian Ocean

1492–93 Columbus becomes first European to sail to the Americas

1493–96 Columbus's second voyage, to the West Indies

1494 Treaty of Tordesillas divides the undiscovered world between Portugal and Spain

1497 Italian John Cabot sails to Newfoundland for the English king

1497–98 Vasco da Gama opens up a new trade route from Europe across the Indian Ocean to India

1498–1500 Columbus's third voyage: he becomes the first European to land in South America

1500

1502–04 Columbus's fourth voyage: he lands in Central America

1519–21 Magellan becomes the first European to sail across the Pacific

1521–22 Sebastián de Elcano completes Magellan's voyage as the first person to sail around the world

1527–28 Pánfilo de Narváez explores the Gulf of Mexico for Spain

1534 Jacques Cartier searches for a Northwest Passage to Asia for the French king, but he discovers Canada instead

1550

1567–69 Álvaro de Mendaña explores the southern Pacific Ocean for Spain

1576 Martin Frobisher explores the Northwest Passage for England

1577–80 Francis Drake sails around the world

1596–98 Dutch navigator Willem Barents explores the Northeast Passage

1600

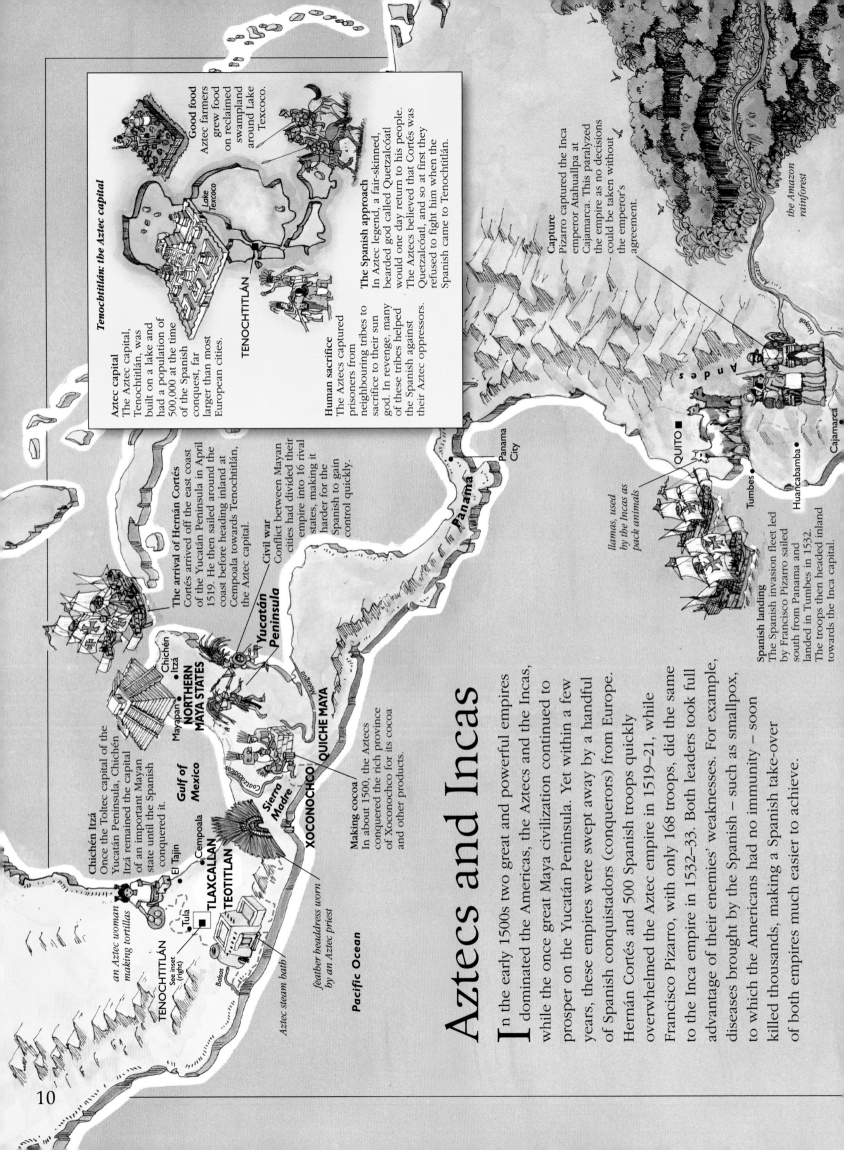

Aztecs and Incas

In the early 1500s two great and powerful empires dominated the Americas, the Aztecs and the Incas, while the once great Maya civilization continued to prosper on the Yucatán Peninsula. Yet within a few years, these empires were swept away by a handful of Spanish conquistadors (conquerors) from Europe. Hernán Cortés and 500 Spanish troops quickly overwhelmed the Aztec empire in 1519–21, while Francisco Pizarro, with only 168 troops, did the same to the Inca empire in 1532–33. Both leaders took full advantage of their enemies' weaknesses. For example, diseases brought by the Spanish – such as smallpox, to which the Americans had no immunity – soon killed thousands, making a Spanish take-over of both empires much easier to achieve.

Tenochtitlán: the Aztec capital

Aztec capital
The Aztec capital, Tenochtitlán, was built on a lake and had a population of 500,000 at the time of the Spanish conquest, far larger than most European cities.

Good food
Aztec farmers grew food on reclaimed swampland around Lake Texcoco.

Lake Texcoco

TENOCHTITLÁN

Human sacrifice
The Aztecs captured prisoners from neighbouring tribes to sacrifice to their sun god. In revenge, many of these tribes helped the Spanish against their Aztec oppressors.

The Spanish approach
In Aztec legend, a fair-skinned, bearded god called Quetzalcóatl would one day return to his people. The Aztecs believed that Cortés was Quetzalcóatl, and so at first they refused to fight him when the Spanish came to Tenochtitlán.

Capture
Pizarro captured the Inca emperor Atahuallpa at Cajamarca. This paralyzed the empire as no decisions could be taken without the emperor's agreement.

the Amazon rainforest

Ucayali

Amazon

Andes

QUITO

Tumbes •

Huancabamba •

Cajamarca •

llamas, used by the Incas as pack animals

Spanish landing
The Spanish invasion fleet led by Francisco Pizarro sailed south from Panama and landed in Tumbes in 1532. The troops then headed inland towards the Inca capital.

Panama City

Panama

Chichén Itzá
Once the Toltec capital of the Yucatán Peninsula, Chichén Itzá remained the capital of an important Mayan state until the Spanish conquered it.

an Aztec woman making tortillas

TENOCHTITLÁN
See inset (right)

TLAXCALLAN
TEOTITLAN

El Tajín •
Cempoala •
Tula •

Gulf of Mexico

Aztec steam bath

feather headdress worn by an Aztec priest

Sierra Madre

Coatzacoalcos

XOCONOCHCO

Pacific Ocean

Making cocoa
In about 1500, the Aztecs conquered the rich province of Xoconochco for its cocoa and other products.

Chichén Itzá •

Mayapan •

NORTHERN MAYA STATES

QUICHE MAYA

Yucatán Peninsula

The arrival of Hernán Cortés
Cortés arrived off the east coast of the Yucatán Peninsula in April 1519. He then sailed around the coast before heading inland at Cempoala towards Tenochtitlán, the Aztec capital.

Civil war
Conflict between Mayan cities had divided their empire into 16 rival states, making it harder for the Spanish to gain control quickly.

Usumacinta

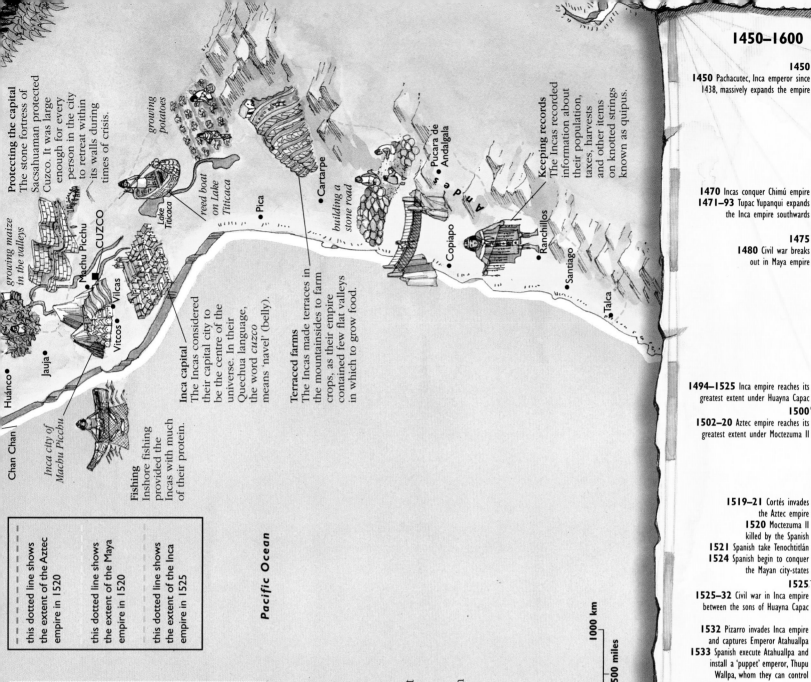

Protecting the capital
The stone fortress of Sacsahuaman protected Cuzco. It was large enough for every person in the city to retreat within its walls during times of crisis.

growing potatoes

growing maize in the valleys

Keeping records
The Incas recorded information about their population, taxes, harvests and other items on knotted strings known as quipus.

reed boat on Lake Titicaca

Lake Titicaca

building a stone road

CUZCO

Machu Picchu

Inca city of Machu Picchu

Chan Chan

Huánco

Jauja

Vilcas

Vitcos

Pica

Cartarpe

Copiapo

Pucara de Andalgala

Ranchillos

Santiago

Talca

Inca capital
The Incas considered their capital city to be the centre of the universe. In their Quechua language, the word *cuzco* means 'navel' (belly).

Terraced farms
The Incas made terraces in the mountainsides to farm crops, as their empire contained few flat valleys in which to grow food.

Fishing
Inshore fishing provided the Incas with much of their protein.

this dotted line shows the extent of the Aztec empire in 1520

this dotted line shows the extent of the Maya empire in 1520

this dotted line shows the extent of the Inca empire in 1525

Pacific Ocean

1000 km
500 miles
0
0

The Spanish conquest

Although few in number, the Spanish were able to conquer the mighty Aztec, Maya and Inca empires because they were much better armed and fought on horses, which were unknown in the Americas at that time. Most importantly, the Spanish were able to exploit their enemies' weaknesses: many local tribes hated the bloodthirsty Aztecs and fought with the Spanish against them, while the Inca empire had not yet recovered from a lengthy civil war. Only the Mayas held out for a long period, as they were divided into 16 different city-states, making it difficult for the Spanish to conquer them all in one go. This picture (above) shows native Americans receiving Christian communion from a Spanish priest.

1450

1450 Pachacutec, Inca emperor since 1438, massively expands the empire

1470 Incas conquer Chimú empire
1471–93 Tupac Yupanqui expands the Inca empire southwards

1475

1480 Civil war breaks out in Maya empire

1494–1525 Inca empire reaches its greatest extent under Huayna Capac

1500

1502–20 Aztec empire reaches its greatest extent under Moctezuma II

1519–21 Cortés invades the Aztec empire
1520 Moctezuma II killed by the Spanish
1521 Spanish take Tenochtitlán
1524 Spanish begin to conquer the Mayan city-states

1525

1525–32 Civil war in Inca empire between the sons of Huayna Capac

1532 Pizarro invades Inca empire and captures Emperor Atahuallpa
1533 Spanish execute Atahuallpa and install a 'puppet' emperor, Thupu Wallpa, whom they can control

1536 Spanish take direct control of the Inca empire

1550

1572 Last Inca resistance crushed in the mountain strongholds

1575

1600 Mayan resistance to the Spanish continues until 1697

1600

Charles V and the Habsburg empire

Charles V of Spain was master of Europe. Born in 1500, he inherited the Rhineland and Netherlands from his Habsburg father, plus Spain and its Italian and American empires from his Spanish grandfather and mother. In 1519 he inherited Habsburg Austria from his grandfather and was elected Holy Roman Emperor, in effect the ruler of Germany. He abdicated (resigned) in 1556 and died in 1558.

Spain and its empire

In the early 1500s Spain, ruled by the Habsburg family of Austria, emerged as the most powerful nation in Europe. The country and its king, Charles V, had gained a large European empire through marriage and inheritance, and then a second empire in the Americas through conquest. Spain became the major Catholic power in Europe and led the fight against the Protestant Reformation (see pages 16–17). Spanish power attracted many enemies and the empire soon proved too big for one person to rule. In 1556 Charles V split his empire in two, giving Spain and its territories to his son, and other lands to his brother.

La Coruña

The Spanish Armada
In 1588 a large fleet left La Coruña to invade England and depose the Protestant queen Elizabeth I. The fleet was defeated by a combination of the English navy and very bad weather.

Don Quixote
The Spanish writer Miguel de Cervantes wrote the classic story of *Don Quixote*. It was published in two parts, in 1605 and 1615.

cork tree

PORTUGAL

The Escorial Palace
Philip II ordered a huge palace to be built outside Madrid, from which to govern his vast European and American empire.

Ebro

MADRID ■

SPAIN

Castile

Taking over Portugal
In 1580 Philip II of Spain defeated the Portuguese at Alcantara and seized the Portuguese throne. Spain held on to Portugal's vast empire until 1640.

Toledo

Alcantara

Tagus

Joint monarchs
In 1469 Ferdinand of Aragon married Isabella of Castile. In 1479 they both succeeded to their thrones and ruled their countries jointly, uniting Spain.

The Morisco revolt
Islamic Moors were converted to Christianity by force in 1492. They rebelled against Spanish rule 70 years later.

Guadiana

Toledo cathedral

LISBON

School of Navigation
In 1416 Prince Henry the Navigator, son of the king of Portugal, opened a navigation school at Sagres to promote exploration and discovery.

Guadalquivir

Córdoba

End of Moorish rule
Ferdinand and Isabella finally drove the Moors out of Granada in 1492, ending 781 years of Muslim rule in Spain.

Seville

Granada

Sagres

Atlantic Ocean

Cadiz

Raiding parties
English privateers (pirates sent by the government) led by Francis Drake regularly raided Spanish ports to seize American treasure and disrupt shipping.

Ceuta

Tangier

Melilla

Coastal forts
The Spaniards built a series of forts along the north African coast, from which to control the western Mediterranean and fight the Ottomans.

North Africa

Heading south
After 1432, Portuguese navigators began to explore the west coast of Africa, setting up trading posts as they sailed further south.

| 0 | | 200 km |
| 0 | | 100 miles |

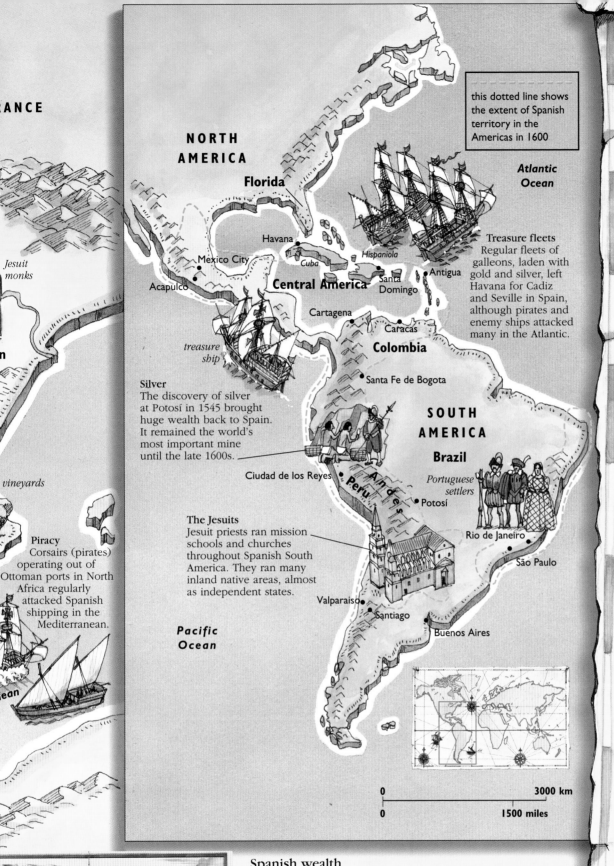

FRANCE

avarre

Jesuit monks

Aragon

vineyards

Piracy
Corsairs (pirates) operating out of Ottoman ports in North Africa regularly attacked Spanish shipping in the Mediterranean.

Mediterranean Sea

Oran

NORTH AMERICA

Florida

Havana

Mexico City

Acapulco

Central America

treasure ship

Cuba

Hispaniola

Santa Domingo

Antigua

Cartagena

Caracas

Colombia

Santa Fe de Bogota

Silver
The discovery of silver at Potosí in 1545 brought huge wealth back to Spain. It remained the world's most important mine until the late 1600s.

Ciudad de los Reyes

Andes
Peru

The Jesuits
Jesuit priests ran mission schools and churches throughout Spanish South America. They ran many inland native areas, almost as independent states.

Pacific Ocean

Valparaiso

Santiago

Buenos Aires

Atlantic Ocean

this dotted line shows the extent of Spanish territory in the Americas in 1600

Treasure fleets
Regular fleets of galleons, laden with gold and silver, left Havana for Cadiz and Seville in Spain, although pirates and enemy ships attacked many in the Atlantic.

SOUTH AMERICA

Brazil

Portuguese settlers

Potosí

Rio de Janeiro

São Paulo

0   **3000 km**

0   **1500 miles**

Spanish wealth

The gold and silver mines of Mexico and Peru brought vast wealth to Spain. Large galleons, accompanied by armed warships, carried the bullion across the Atlantic. Despite these precautions, pirates and enemy ships, particularly from England and Holland, often attacked the fleets. This wealth enabled Spain to dominate Europe, as it could afford to pay for large armies, but it also caused prices to rise at home, eventually ruining the Spanish economy. This picture shows a plan of the silver mines at Potosí, in modern-day Bolivia.

The Renaissance:
A world of new learning

The Renaissance – a French word meaning 'rebirth' – was an artistic, cultural and intellectual movement that influenced all the arts and sciences. Renaissance artists and scholars looked back to the art and learning of classical Rome and Greece for their inspiration, reviving the past in order to develop and explore new ideas and methods. This new approach became known as 'humanism', because it encouraged people to achieve things for themselves rather than simply accept what they were taught to be true. The Renaissance began in Italy during the 14th century and reached its height during the 15th and 16th centuries, spreading across all of western and northern Europe.

Scientific invention
A 'Renaissance man' or 'universal man' was someone who could do many things. One such person was Leonardo da Vinci (1452–1519), who, as well as being an artist and a sculptor, drew plans for a helicopter (above), flying machine, and tank. He also dissected human bodies to find out more about how we move and function.

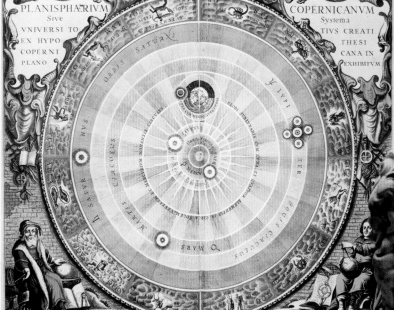

Renaissance art
Renaissance artists depicted people and landscapes in a highly natural way, studying anatomy and perspective to make their paintings more realistic. Michelangelo (1475–1564) was perhaps the greatest Renaissance artist, creating life-like sculptures, such as his *David* (left), and vast paintings such as the ceiling of the Sistine Chapel in Rome, Italy.

Astronomy
The Renaissance encouraged scientists to explore new ideas and to challenge existing beliefs. In 1543 the Polish astronomer Nicolaus Copernicus (1473–1543) proposed that the Sun is at the centre of the solar system and all the planets revolve around it. This shocked many people, because their religious teachings had always insisted that the Earth was at the centre of the universe. The chart above shows the arrangement suggested by Copernicus.

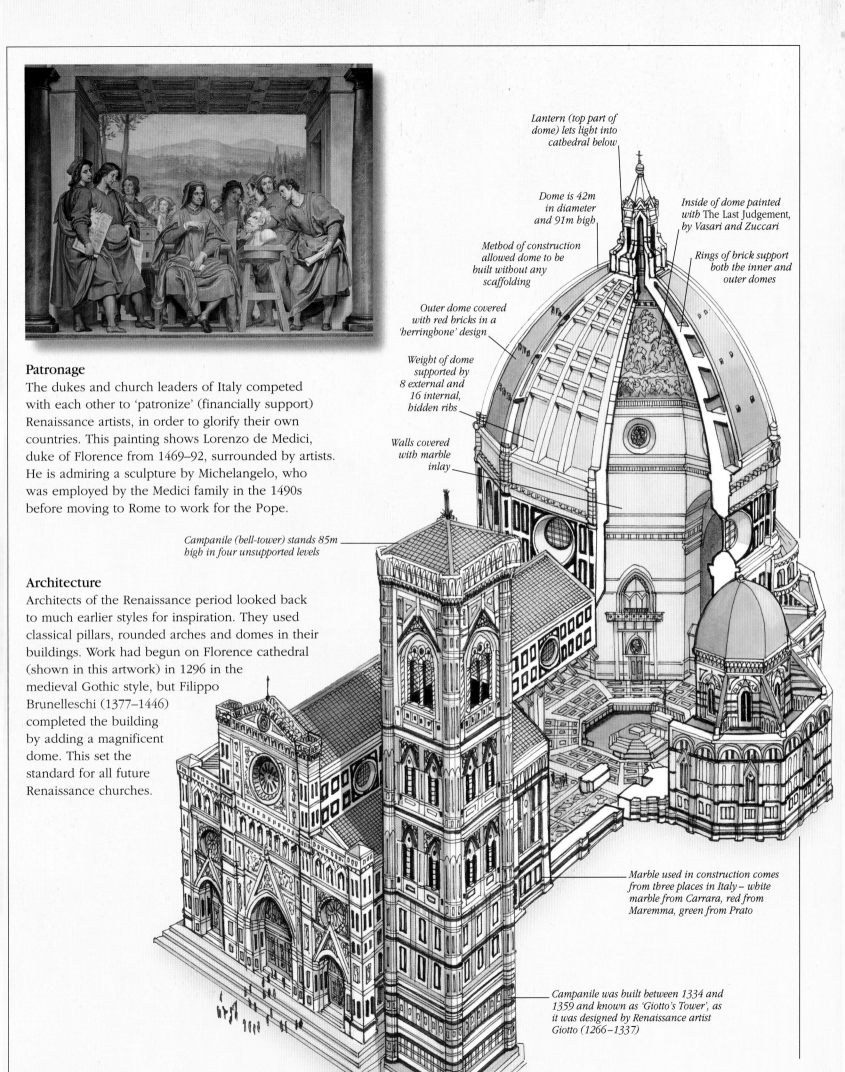

Patronage

The dukes and church leaders of Italy competed with each other to 'patronize' (financially support) Renaissance artists, in order to glorify their own countries. This painting shows Lorenzo de Medici, duke of Florence from 1469–92, surrounded by artists. He is admiring a sculpture by Michelangelo, who was employed by the Medici family in the 1490s before moving to Rome to work for the Pope.

Campanile (bell-tower) stands 85m high in four unsupported levels

Architecture

Architects of the Renaissance period looked back to much earlier styles for inspiration. They used classical pillars, rounded arches and domes in their buildings. Work had begun on Florence cathedral (shown in this artwork) in 1296 in the medieval Gothic style, but Filippo Brunelleschi (1377–1446) completed the building by adding a magnificent dome. This set the standard for all future Renaissance churches.

Lantern (top part of dome) lets light into cathedral below

Dome is 42m in diameter and 91m high

Inside of dome painted with The Last Judgement, by Vasari and Zuccari

Method of construction allowed dome to be built without any scaffolding

Rings of brick support both the inner and outer domes

Outer dome covered with red bricks in a 'herringbone' design

Weight of dome supported by 8 external and 16 internal, hidden ribs

Walls covered with marble inlay

Marble used in construction comes from three places in Italy – white marble from Carrara, red from Maremma, green from Prato

Campanile was built between 1334 and 1359 and known as 'Giotto's Tower', as it was designed by Renaissance artist Giotto (1266–1337)

The Reformation

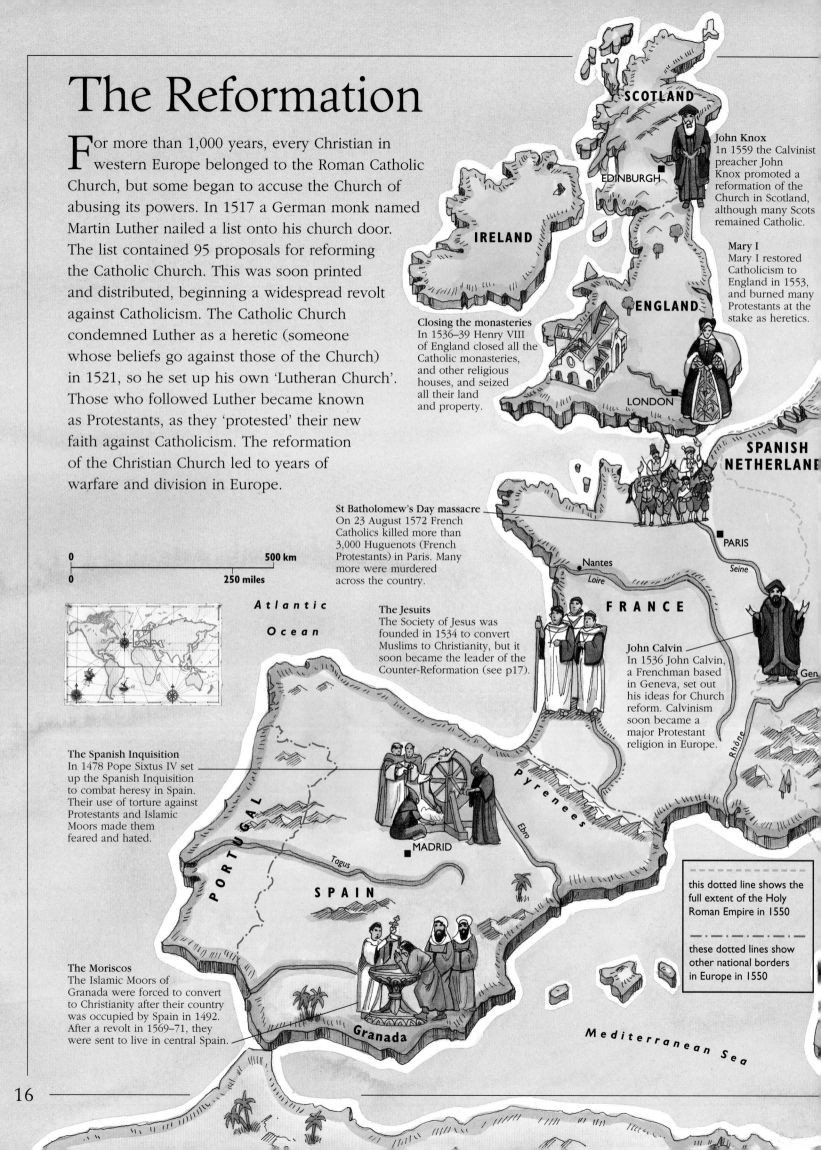

For more than 1,000 years, every Christian in western Europe belonged to the Roman Catholic Church, but some began to accuse the Church of abusing its powers. In 1517 a German monk named Martin Luther nailed a list onto his church door. The list contained 95 proposals for reforming the Catholic Church. This was soon printed and distributed, beginning a widespread revolt against Catholicism. The Catholic Church condemned Luther as a heretic (someone whose beliefs go against those of the Church) in 1521, so he set up his own 'Lutheran Church'. Those who followed Luther became known as Protestants, as they 'protested' their new faith against Catholicism. The reformation of the Christian Church led to years of warfare and division in Europe.

John Knox
In 1559 the Calvinist preacher John Knox promoted a reformation of the Church in Scotland, although many Scots remained Catholic.

Mary I
Mary I restored Catholicism to England in 1553, and burned many Protestants at the stake as heretics.

Closing the monasteries
In 1536–39 Henry VIII of England closed all the Catholic monasteries, and other religious houses, and seized all their land and property.

St Batholomew's Day massacre
On 23 August 1572 French Catholics killed more than 3,000 Huguenots (French Protestants) in Paris. Many more were murdered across the country.

The Jesuits
The Society of Jesus was founded in 1534 to convert Muslims to Christianity, but it soon became the leader of the Counter-Reformation (see p17).

John Calvin
In 1536 John Calvin, a Frenchman based in Geneva, set out his ideas for Church reform. Calvinism soon became a major Protestant religion in Europe.

The Spanish Inquisition
In 1478 Pope Sixtus IV set up the Spanish Inquisition to combat heresy in Spain. Their use of torture against Protestants and Islamic Moors made them feared and hated.

The Moriscos
The Islamic Moors of Granada were forced to convert to Christianity after their country was occupied by Spain in 1492. After a revolt in 1569–71, they were sent to live in central Spain.

this dotted line shows the full extent of the Holy Roman Empire in 1550

these dotted lines show other national borders in Europe in 1550

0 500 km
0 250 miles

SCOTLAND
EDINBURGH
IRELAND
ENGLAND
LONDON
SPANISH NETHERLAND
PARIS
Seine
Nantes
Loire
FRANCE
Gen
Rhône
Pyrenees
Ebro
PORTUGAL
MADRID
Tagus
SPAIN
Granada
Atlantic Ocean
Mediterranean Sea

North
Sea

NORWAY

DENMARK

SWEDEN

Baltic Sea

Gutenberg's printing press, developed in the 1440s

radical preachers

German Catholic church in flames

Elbe

Wittenberg

Saxony

Germany

Worms

Rhine

HOLY ROMAN EMPIRE

SWISS CONFEDERATION

Augsburg

Zürich

Danube

Bavaria

Council of Trent
Catholic officials met at Trent three times after 1545.

Trent

Austria

HUNGARY

A l p s

Po

VENICE

OTTOMAN EMPIRE

PAPAL STATES

ROME

St Peter's Basilica in Rome, Italy

The Pope
As a result of the Reformation, Rome's role as the headquarters of the Christian Church was reduced, but the Pope remained an important figure in Europe for many years.

Martin Luther

Martin Luther (1483–1546), pictured here in dark robes, was an Augustinian friar and professor of theology at Wittenberg University in Saxony. He objected to many aspects of Catholic belief and practice, but wanted at first to reform the Church, not divide it. When this proved impossible, he set up his own reformed church.

Corpernicus

In 1531 Copernicus, a Polish astronomer, demonstrated that the planets move around the Sun, and not around the Earth. This went against the teachings of the Catholic Church.

The 95 Theses

In 1517 Martin Luther nailed 95 proposals for Catholic reform to the door of his church in Wittenberg, Saxony.

POLAND

Expelling Protestants

In the late 1550s, Protestants were thrown out of Bavaria and Austria as the Catholic Church regained control. Poland, too, became Catholic again.

The Counter-Reformation

From 1545 to 1563, the Roman Catholic Church met at Trent in the Alps to reform the Church and help it fight back against Protestantism. The Counter-Reformation saw great changes in practice, while religious buildings in the new Baroque style of architecture – such as St Peter's Basilica in Rome, Italy (above) – helped to attract people back into the Catholic Church.

1510

1517 Martin Luther nails 95 proposals for Catholic reform onto his church door in Wittenberg, Saxony

1520

1521 Luther presents his ideas for reform to the Holy Roman Emperor at the Diet (council) of Worms
1523 In Zürich, Ulrich Zwingli proposes 67 reforms of the Catholic Church
1524 Religious warfare breaks out in Germany as peasants rise up in revolt
1525 Lutheranism is state religion of Saxony and many other German states

1530

1531 Copernicus suggests the Sun, not Earth, is at the centre of the universe
1534 Society of Jesus (Jesuits) forms
1534 Henry VIII of England breaks away from the Catholic Church when it refuses him a divorce
1536 John Calvin sets out ideas for religious reforms in his book, 'Institutes'
1536–39 Henry VIII closes monasteries

1540

1541 John Calvin begins to organize a strict Protestant church in Geneva

1544 Sweden converts to Lutheranism
1545–63 Roman Catholic Church meets three times at Trent, in the Alps, to launch the Counter-Reformation against Protestant churches

1550

1553–58 England briefly becomes Catholic again under Queen Mary I
1555 After years of war, Holy Roman Emperor agrees the Peace of Augsburg, giving each ruler within the empire the right to choose their own state religion

1558 Elizabeth I comes to the throne and restores Protestantism to England

1560

1560 Scottish parliament declares Scotland to be a Protestant nation
1562–80 French wars of religion divide the country

1566 Dutch Protestants rise in revolt against Spanish Catholic rulers

1570

1572 Thousands of French Huguenots (Protestants) are massacred by Catholics

1580

1589 The Huguenot Henry Navarre becomes king Henry IV of France
1590

1593 Henry IV of France becomes a Catholic

1598 Edict of Nantes grants religious toleration to Huguenots in France

1600

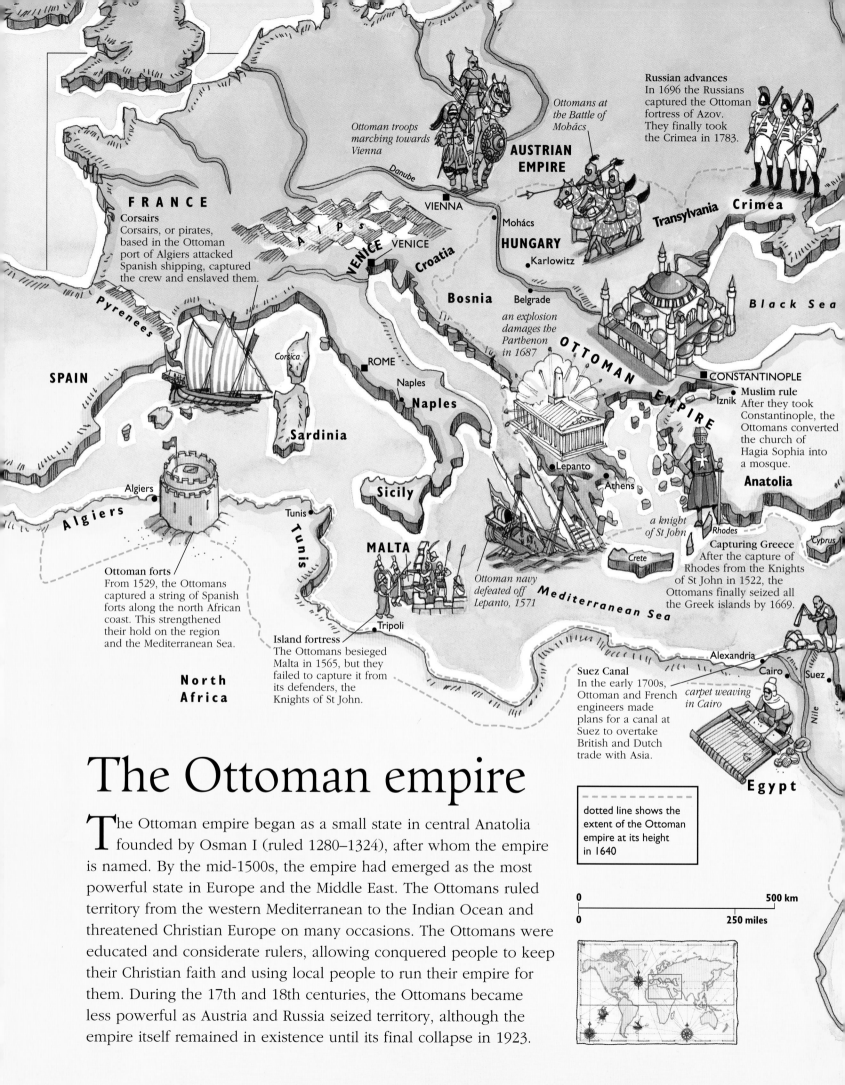

Russian advances
In 1696 the Russians captured the Ottoman fortress of Azov. They finally took the Crimea in 1783.

Ottoman troops marching towards Vienna

Ottomans at the Battle of Mohács

AUSTRIAN EMPIRE

Danube

VIENNA

Mohács

Transylvania

Crimea

F R A N C E

Corsairs
Corsairs, or pirates, based in the Ottoman port of Algiers attacked Spanish shipping, captured the crew and enslaved them.

A L P S

VENICE   VENICE

HUNGARY

Karlowitz

Croatia

Bosnia

Belgrade

an explosion damages the Parthenon in 1687

O T T O M A N

Black Sea

P y r e n e e s

SPAIN

Corsica

ROME

Naples

Naples

Sardinia

CONSTANTINOPLE

Muslim rule
After they took Constantinople, the Ottomans converted the church of Hagia Sophia into a mosque.

Iznik

E M P I R E

Anatolia

Lepanto

Athens

a knight of St John

Rhodes

Cyprus

Algiers

A l g i e r s

Tunis

Sicily

T u n i s

MALTA

Ottoman forts
From 1529, the Ottomans captured a string of Spanish forts along the north African coast. This strengthened their hold on the region and the Mediterranean Sea.

Island fortress
The Ottomans besieged Malta in 1565, but they failed to capture it from its defenders, the Knights of St John.

Tripoli

Ottoman navy defeated off Lepanto, 1571

Crete

M e d i t e r r a n e a n S e a

Capturing Greece
After the capture of Rhodes from the Knights of St John in 1522, the Ottomans finally seized all the Greek islands by 1669.

North Africa

Suez Canal
In the early 1700s, Ottoman and French engineers made plans for a canal at Suez to overtake British and Dutch trade with Asia.

Alexandria

Cairo   Suez

carpet weaving in Cairo

Nile

Egypt

The Ottoman empire

The Ottoman empire began as a small state in central Anatolia founded by Osman I (ruled 1280–1324), after whom the empire is named. By the mid-1500s, the empire had emerged as the most powerful state in Europe and the Middle East. The Ottomans ruled territory from the western Mediterranean to the Indian Ocean and threatened Christian Europe on many occasions. The Ottomans were educated and considerate rulers, allowing conquered people to keep their Christian faith and using local people to run their empire for them. During the 17th and 18th centuries, the Ottomans became less powerful as Austria and Russia seized territory, although the empire itself remained in existence until its final collapse in 1923.

dotted line shows the extent of the Ottoman empire at its height in 1640

0   500 km

0   250 miles

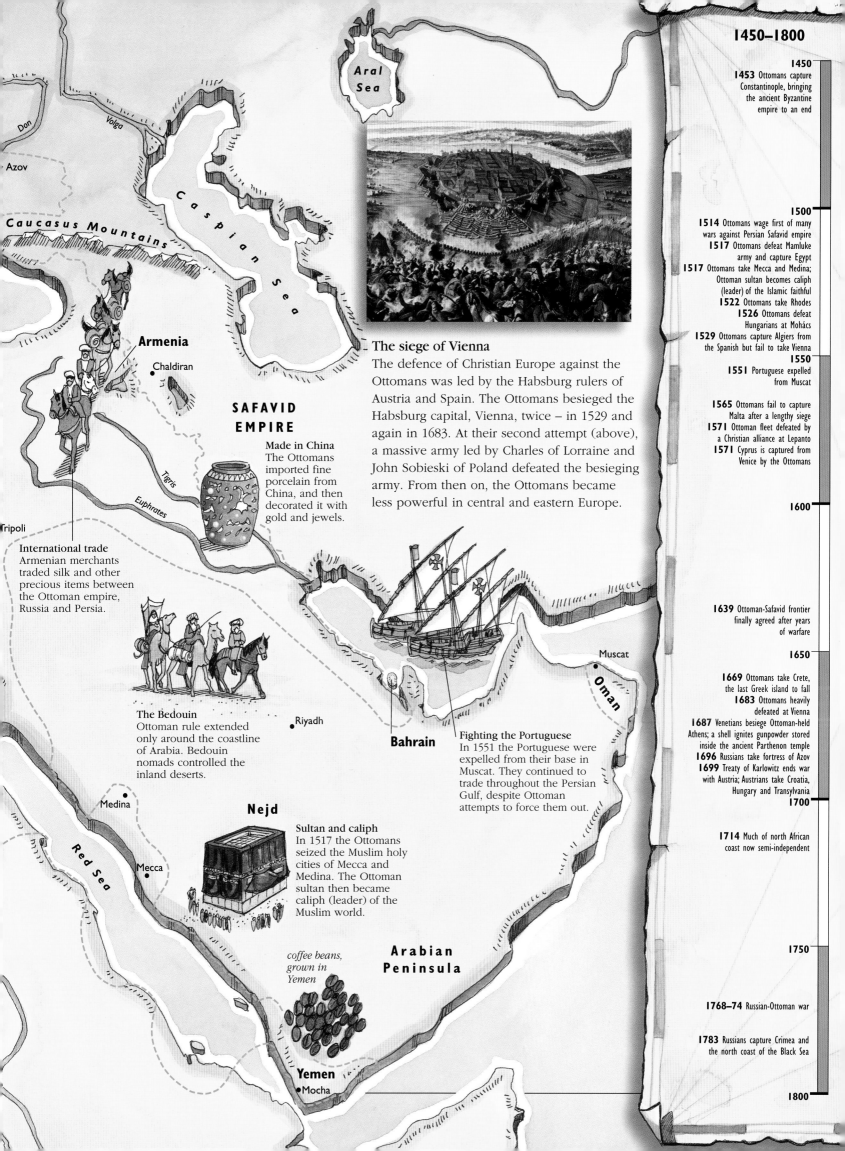

Map labels and locations

Aral Sea

Don

Volga

Azov

Caspian Sea

Caucasus Mountains

Armenia

• Chaldiran

SAFAVID EMPIRE

Tigris

Euphrates

Tripoli

• Riyadh

Bahrain

Muscat •

Oman

• Medina

Nejd

Red Sea

Mecca •

Arabian Peninsula

coffee beans, grown in Yemen

Yemen

• Mocha

The siege of Vienna

The defence of Christian Europe against the Ottomans was led by the Habsburg rulers of Austria and Spain. The Ottomans besieged the Habsburg capital, Vienna, twice – in 1529 and again in 1683. At their second attempt (above), a massive army led by Charles of Lorraine and John Sobieski of Poland defeated the besieging army. From then on, the Ottomans became less powerful in central and eastern Europe.

Made in China
The Ottomans imported fine porcelain from China, and then decorated it with gold and jewels.

International trade
Armenian merchants traded silk and other precious items between the Ottoman empire, Russia and Persia.

The Bedouin
Ottoman rule extended only around the coastline of Arabia. Bedouin nomads controlled the inland deserts.

Fighting the Portuguese
In 1551 the Portuguese were expelled from their base in Muscat. They continued to trade throughout the Persian Gulf, despite Ottoman attempts to force them out.

Sultan and caliph
In 1517 the Ottomans seized the Muslim holy cities of Mecca and Medina. The Ottoman sultan then became caliph (leader) of the Muslim world.

1450–1800

1450

1453 Ottomans capture Constantinople, bringing the ancient Byzantine empire to an end

1500

1514 Ottomans wage first of many wars against Persian Safavid empire
1517 Ottomans defeat Mamluke army and capture Egypt
1517 Ottomans take Mecca and Medina; Ottoman sultan becomes caliph (leader) of the Islamic faithful
1522 Ottomans take Rhodes
1526 Ottomans defeat Hungarians at Mohács
1529 Ottomans capture Algiers from the Spanish but fail to take Vienna

1550

1551 Portuguese expelled from Muscat

1565 Ottomans fail to capture Malta after a lengthy siege
1571 Ottoman fleet defeated by a Christian alliance at Lepanto
1571 Cyprus is captured from Venice by the Ottomans

1600

1639 Ottoman-Safavid frontier finally agreed after years of warfare

1650

1669 Ottomans take Crete, the last Greek island to fall
1683 Ottomans heavily defeated at Vienna
1687 Venetians besiege Ottoman-held Athens; a shell ignites gunpowder stored inside the ancient Parthenon temple
1696 Russians take fortress of Azov
1699 Treaty of Karlowitz ends war with Austria; Austrians take Croatia, Hungary and Transylvania

1700

1714 Much of north African coast now semi-independent

1750

1768–74 Russian-Ottoman war

1783 Russians capture Crimea and the north coast of the Black Sea

1800

The Mughal empire

In the late 1400s, the Mughals, descendants of the famous Mongol leader Timur, were driven out of central Asia by the Mongol Tatars. They moved southwards and began to raid India, mounting a full-scale invasion in 1526. They soon conquered northern India and by 1600 were advancing south into the Deccan. A century later they controlled all but the far south. The Mughals were good administrators and, although Muslims, allowed their Hindu and Sikh subjects to worship freely. In the 1700s the Mughal empire came under attack from the Hindu Marathas of the west coast, while the French and British also gained territory. By 1800 the British had defeated the French and dominated Mughal India.

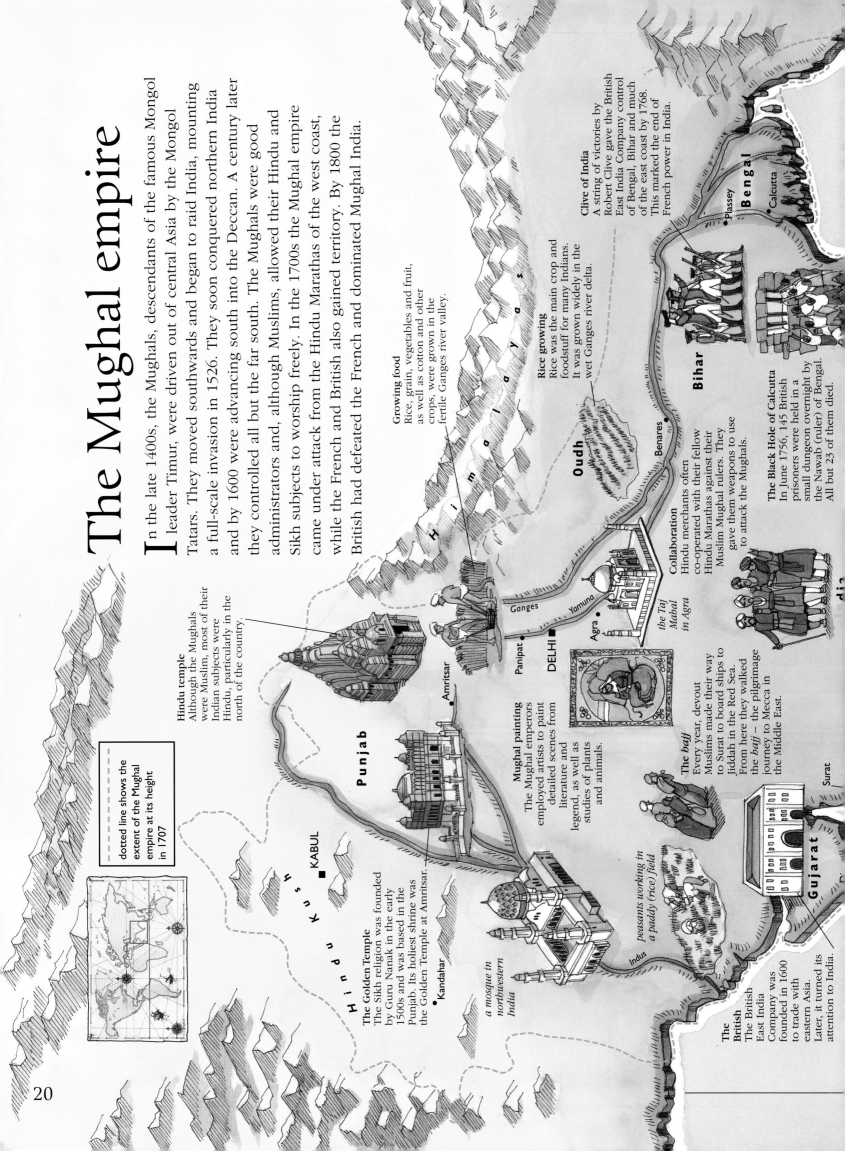

dotted line shows the extent of the Mughal empire at its height in 1707

Hindu temple
Although the Mughals were Muslim, most of their Indian subjects were Hindu, particularly in the north of the country.

The Golden Temple
The Sikh religion was founded by Guru Nanak in the early 1500s and was based in the Punjab. Its holiest shrine was the Golden Temple at Amritsar.

a mosque in northwestern India

The British
The British East India Company was founded in 1600 to trade with eastern Asia. Later, it turned its attention to India.

Mughal painting
The Mughal emperors employed artists to paint detailed scenes from literature and legend, as well as studies of plants and animals.

The hajj
Every year, devout Muslims made their way to Surat to board ships to Jiddah in the Red Sea. From here they walked the *hajj* – the pilgrimage journey to Mecca in the Middle East.

peasants working in a paddy (rice) field

Growing food
Rice, grain, vegetables and fruit, as well as cotton and other crops, were grown in the fertile Ganges river valley.

Rice growing
Rice was the main crop and foodstuff for many Indians. It was grown widely in the wet Ganges river delta.

Collaboration
Hindu merchants often co-operated with their fellow Hindu Marathas against their Muslim Mughal rulers. They gave them weapons to use to attack the Mughals.

the Taj Mahal in Agra

The Black Hole of Calcutta
In June 1756, 145 British prisoners were held in a small dungeon overnight by the Nawab (ruler) of Bengal. All but 23 of them died.

Clive of India
A string of victories by Robert Clive gave the British East India Company control of Bengal, Bihar and much of the east coast by 1768. This marked the end of French power in India.

Hindu Kush

KABUL

Kandahar

Punjab

Amritsar

Panipat

DELHI

Agra

Yamuna

Ganges

H i m a l a y a s

Benares

Oudh

Bihar

Bengal

Plassey

Calcutta

Indus

Gujarat

Surat

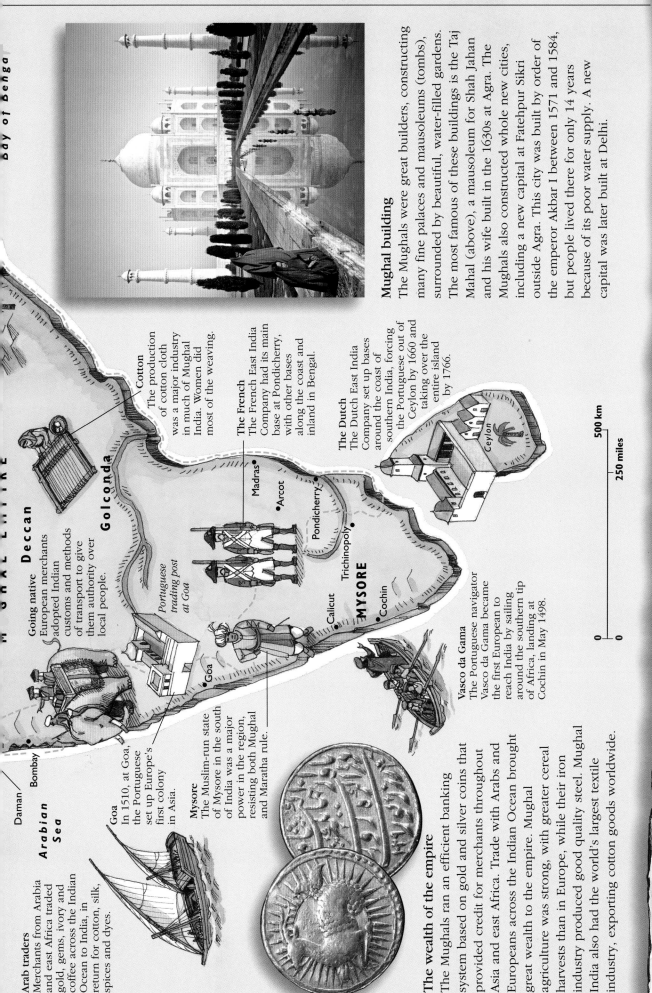

Mughal building

The Mughals were great builders, constructing many fine palaces and mausoleums (tombs), surrounded by beautiful, water-filled gardens. The most famous of these buildings is the Taj Mahal (above), a mausoleum for Shah Jahan and his wife built in the 1630s at Agra. The Mughals also constructed whole new cities, including a new capital at Fatehpur Sikri outside Agra. This city was built by order of the emperor Akbar I between 1571 and 1584, but people lived there for only 14 years because of its poor water supply. A new capital was later built at Delhi.

Cotton
The production of cotton cloth was a major industry in much of Mughal India. Women did most of the weaving.

The French
The French East India Company had its main base at Pondicherry, with other bases along the coast and inland in Bengal.

The Dutch
The Dutch East India Company set up bases around the coast of southern India, forcing the Portuguese out of Ceylon by 1660 and taking over the entire island by 1766.

Going native
European merchants adopted Indian customs and methods of transport to give them authority over local people.

Arab traders
Merchants from Arabia and east Africa traded gold, gems, ivory and coffee across the Indian Ocean to India, in return for cotton, silk, spices and dyes.

Goa
In 1510, at Goa, the Portuguese set up Europe's first colony in Asia.

Mysore
The Muslim-run state of Mysore in the south of India was a major power in the region, resisting both Mughal and Maratha rule.

Vasco da Gama
The Portuguese navigator Vasco da Gama became the first European to reach India by sailing around the southern tip of Africa, landing at Cochin in May 1498.

Portuguese trading post at Goa

MUGHAL EMPIRE
Deccan
Golconda
Arabian Sea
Daman
Bombay
Goa
Calicut
Cochin
MYSORE
Trichinopoly
Pondicherry
Arcot
Madras
Ceylon

500 km
250 miles
0
0

The wealth of the empire

The Mughals ran an efficient banking system based on gold and silver coins that provided credit for merchants throughout Asia and east Africa. Trade with Arabs and Europeans across the Indian Ocean brought great wealth to the empire. Mughal agriculture was strong, with greater cereal harvests than in Europe, while their iron industry produced good quality steel. Mughal India also had the world's largest textile industry, exporting cotton goods worldwide.

1500

1501–30 Reign of Babur, first Mughal emperor
1504 Mughals conquer the region around Kabul
1510 Portuguese set up a trading post at Goa, with others at Diu and Daman
1519 Mughals' first raid on India
1526 Full-scale Mughal invasion of India

1539–56 Suri Afghans of Bihar rebel and reclaim a lot of territory from the Mughals

1550

1556–1605 Reign of Akbar I

1572 Mughals conquer Gujarat, giving them access to the sea
1576 Mughals conquer Bengal, India's wealthiest territory

1600

1600 British East India Co founded
1602 Dutch East India Co founded
1605 Mughals advance south into the Deccan
1612 British East India Co defeats a Portuguese fleet at Surat

1628–58 Reign of Shah Jahan, who ordered the building of the Taj Mahal
1639–48 New capital city constructed by order of Shah Jahan at Shahjahanabad (Delhi)
1647–80 Led by Sivaji, Hindu Marathas raid Mughal India

1650

1655–60 Dutch seize bases in Ceylon from Portuguese
1658–1707 Reign of Aurangzeb: Mughal empire at its greatest extent
1661 British East India Co establishes base at Bombay
1664 French East India Co set up

1687 Mughals capture southern state of Golconda

1700

1708 Marathas begin to conquer the Deccan

1739 Persian troops sack Mughal capital of Delhi
1740 War between Marathas and Mughals in southern India draws in the French and the British

1750

1751, 52 British under Robert Clive score decisive victories against the French at Arcot and Trichinopoly
1757 Clive defeats Mughal Nawab (ruler) of Bengal at Plassey
1761 Maratha power ends after massive defeat outside Delhi by an Afghan army that later withdraws from India
1761 British seize Pondicherry, ending French power in India
1775 British control all of Bengal and Bihar
by 1800 Mughal empire survives in name only

1800

The Tudors and Stuarts

Years of warfare in England between rival royal houses ended in 1485 when Henry VII became the first Tudor king. The Tudors were strong rulers who brought peace and prosperity to the country. Under Henry VIII, England broke away from Rome, and the Catholic Church, and became increasingly Protestant. In 1603 the last Tudor monarch, Elizabeth I, died. Elizabeth was succeeded by the Scottish king James VI, of the Stuart family, who united England and Scotland for the first time. But the Stuarts were weak kings. One of them, Charles I, was executed following a civil war, and another, James II (James VII of Scotland), was driven into exile because he was a Catholic. Overseas trade, however, was slowly making Britain one of the wealthiest nations in Europe.

The English Civil War: a war of three kingdoms
Charles I was king of England, Scotland and Ireland. Each country had its own parliament, church and laws. Charles believed he had a "divine right to rule", given to him by God, but his religious policies attracted opposition. Rebellion broke out in Scotland in 1639, then in Ireland in 1641, before king and parliament clashed in England in 1642. Civil war raged in all three kingdoms before Charles was executed by the English parliament, in 1649, for waging war on his people. From 1649 to 1660 Britain was a republic (a nation without a monarch) for the only time in its history.

The Spanish Armada
Defeated in August 1588 (see p23), the Spanish Armada was forced to sail around the rocky north and west coasts of Ireland and Scotland, where many ships were wrecked in storms.

Irish rebellions
Ireland was the only part of the British Isles to remain Catholic. This led to many rebellions against Ireland's Protestant and English rulers.

Atlantic Ocean

Union of the crowns
In 1603 the Stuart king of Scotland, James VI, became King James I of England. This united the two crowns, but both nations remained independent.

Suspicious murder
Lord Darnley, husband of Mary, Queen of Scots, was killed in an explosion in Edinburgh in 1567. Mary was accused of being involved, but nothing was proved.

Flodden Field
The English defeat of the Scots at Flodden Field in 1513 weakened Scotland greatly, and put it at the mercy of the English for the rest of the century.

North Sea

SCOTLAND

■EDINBURGH

Tweed

•Flodden

•Londonderry

Ulster

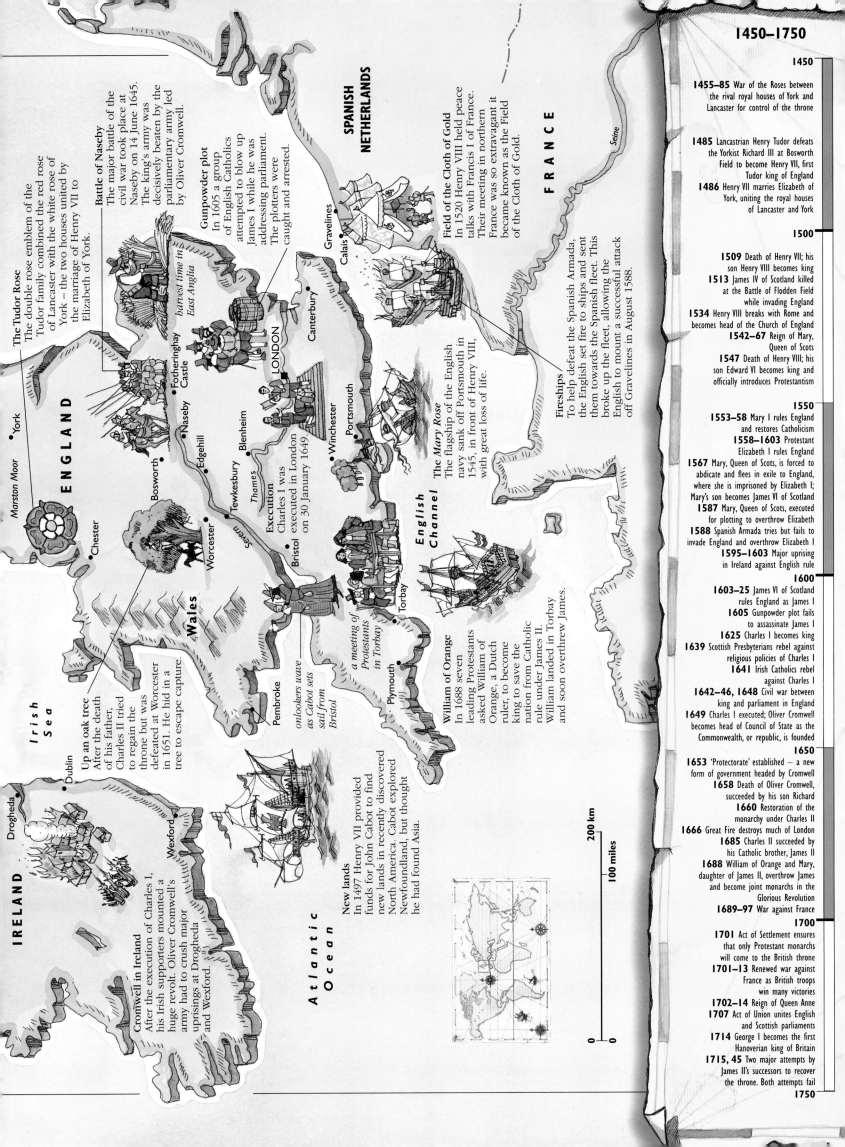

SPANISH NETHERLANDS

FRANCE

Seine

The Tudor Rose
The double rose emblem of the Tudor family combined the red rose of Lancaster with the white rose of York – the two houses united by the marriage of Henry VII to Elizabeth of York.

Battle of Naseby
The major battle of the civil war took place at Naseby on 14 June 1645. The king's army was decisively beaten by the parliamentary army led by Oliver Cromwell.

Gunpowder plot
In 1605 a group of English Catholics attempted to blow up James I while he was addressing parliament. The plotters were caught and arrested.

Field of the Cloth of Gold
In 1520 Henry VIII held peace talks with Francis I of France. Their meeting in northern France was so extravagant it became known as the Field of the Cloth of Gold.

Fireships
To help defeat the Spanish Armada, the English set fire to ships and sent them towards the Spanish fleet. This broke up the fleet, allowing the English to mount a successful attack off Gravelines in August 1588.

Gravelines
Calais
Canterbury
LONDON
Fotheringhay Castle
harvest time in East Anglia

ENGLAND
Marston Moor
York
Bosworth
Naseby
Edgehill
Blenheim
Tewkesbury
Worcester
Chester
Severn
Thames
Winchester
Portsmouth

The Mary Rose
The flagship of the English navy sank off Portsmouth in 1545, in front of Henry VIII, with great loss of life.

Execution
Charles I was executed in London on 30 January 1649.

Wales

English Channel

Torbay
Plymouth

a meeting of Protestants in Torbay

William of Orange
In 1688 seven leading Protestants asked William of Orange, a Dutch ruler, to become king to save the nation from Catholic rule under James II. William landed in Torbay and soon overthrew James.

Irish Sea

Up an oak tree
After the death of his father, Charles II tried to regain the throne but was defeated at Worcester in 1651. He hid in a tree to escape capture.

onlookers wave as Cabot sets sail from Bristol

Pembroke

Dublin

Cromwell in Ireland
After the execution of Charles I, his Irish supporters mounted a huge revolt. Oliver Cromwell's army had to crush major uprisings at Drogheda and Wexford.

IRELAND
Drogheda
Wexford

Atlantic Ocean

New lands
In 1497 Henry VII provided funds for John Cabot to find new lands in recently discovered North America. Cabot explored Newfoundland, but thought he had found Asia.

200 km
100 miles
0

1450–1750

1450

1455–85 War of the Roses between the rival royal houses of York and Lancaster for control of the throne

1485 Lancastrian Henry Tudor defeats the Yorkist Richard III at Bosworth Field to become Henry VII, first Tudor king of England
1486 Henry VII marries Elizabeth of York, uniting the royal houses of Lancaster and York

1500

1509 Death of Henry VII; his son Henry VIII becomes king
1513 James IV of Scotland killed at the Battle of Flodden Field while invading England
1534 Henry VIII breaks with Rome and becomes head of the Church of England
1542–67 Reign of Mary, Queen of Scots
1547 Death of Henry VIII; his son Edward VI becomes king and officially introduces Protestantism

1550

1553–58 Mary I rules England and restores Catholicism
1558–1603 Protestant Elizabeth I rules England
1567 Mary, Queen of Scots, is forced to abdicate and flees in exile to England, where she is imprisoned by Elizabeth I; Mary's son becomes James VI of Scotland
1587 Mary, Queen of Scots, executed for plotting to overthrow Elizabeth
1588 Spanish Armada tries but fails to invade England and overthrow Elizabeth I
1595–1603 Major uprising in Ireland against English rule

1600

1603–25 James VI of Scotland rules England as James I
1605 Gunpowder plot fails to assassinate James I
1625 Charles I becomes king
1639 Scottish Presbyterians rebel against religious policies of Charles I
1641 Irish Catholics rebel against Charles I
1642–46, 1648 Civil war between king and parliament in England
1649 Charles I executed; Oliver Cromwell becomes head of Council of State as the Commonwealth, or republic, is founded

1650

1653 'Protectorate' established — a new form of government headed by Cromwell
1658 Death of Oliver Cromwell, succeeded by his son Richard
1660 Restoration of the monarchy under Charles II
1666 Great Fire destroys much of London
1685 Charles II succeeded by his Catholic brother, James II
1688 William of Orange and Mary, daughter of James II, overthrow James and become joint monarchs in the Glorious Revolution
1689–97 War against France

1700

1701 Act of Settlement ensures that only Protestant monarchs will come to the British throne
1701–13 Renewed war against France as British troops win many victories
1702–14 Reign of Queen Anne
1707 Act of Union unites English and Scottish parliaments
1714 George I becomes the first Hanoverian king of Britain
1715, 45 Two major attempts by James II's successors to recover the throne. Both attempts fail

1750

Divided Europe

After the religious turmoil of the Reformation, a brief period of peace descended on Europe in the 1550s. Differences between Protestants and Catholics continued to divide the continent, however, causing civil war in France and a revolt in the Netherlands against Spanish rule. A major conflict also broke out for control of the Baltic Sea. In 1618, Protestant-Catholic rivalries in Germany led to a war that soon spread across the rest of Europe. By the end of the war, Germany was devastated, Spain lost its leadership of Catholic Europe to France, Sweden dominated northern Europe and the Baltic, and the Dutch were independent and wealthy.

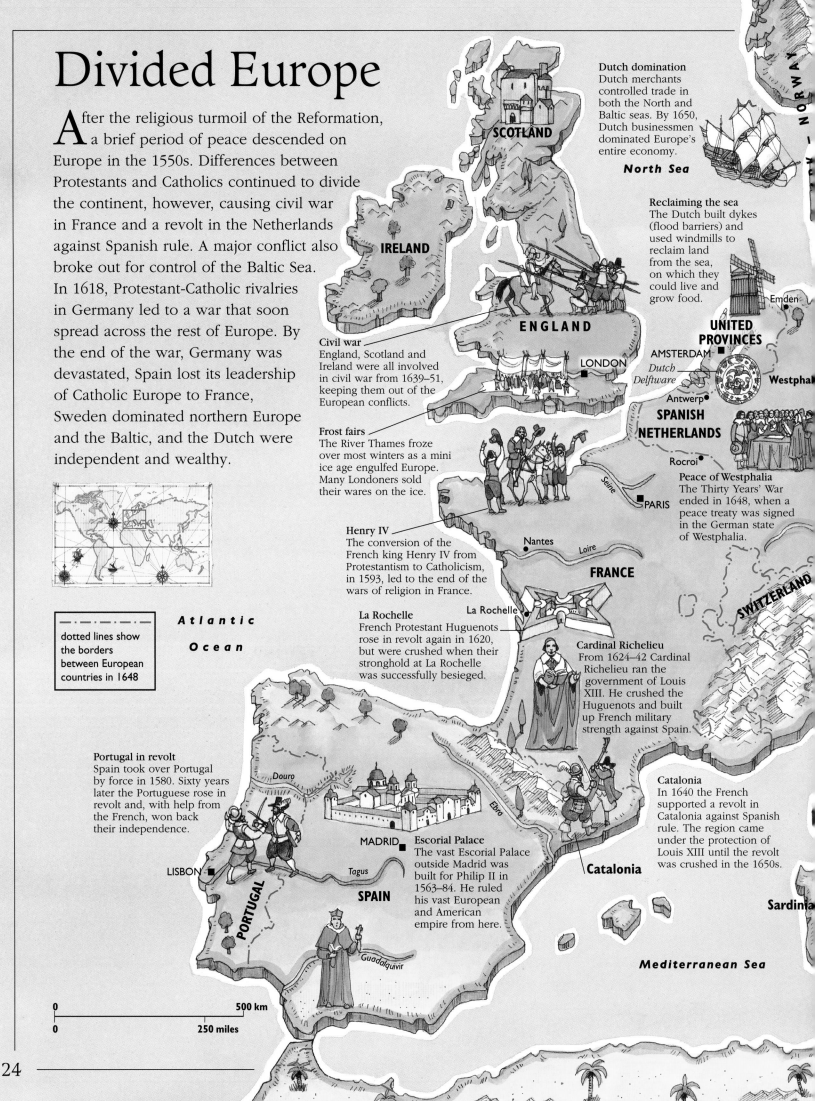

dotted lines show the borders between European countries in 1648

Atlantic Ocean

SCOTLAND

IRELAND

ENGLAND

LONDON

Civil war
England, Scotland and Ireland were all involved in civil war from 1639–51, keeping them out of the European conflicts.

Frost fairs
The River Thames froze over most winters as a mini ice age engulfed Europe. Many Londoners sold their wares on the ice.

Henry IV
The conversion of the French king Henry IV from Protestantism to Catholicism, in 1593, led to the end of the wars of religion in France.

Nantes

Loire

La Rochelle
French Protestant Huguenots rose in revolt again in 1620, but were crushed when their stronghold at La Rochelle was successfully besieged.

La Rochelle

FRANCE

Seine

PARIS

Dutch domination
Dutch merchants controlled trade in both the North and Baltic seas. By 1650, Dutch businessmen dominated Europe's entire economy.

North Sea

Reclaiming the sea
The Dutch built dykes (flood barriers) and used windmills to reclaim land from the sea, on which they could live and grow food.

Emden

UNITED PROVINCES

AMSTERDAM

Dutch Delftware

Westphal

Antwerp

SPANISH NETHERLANDS

Rocroi

Peace of Westphalia
The Thirty Years' War ended in 1648, when a peace treaty was signed in the German state of Westphalia.

SWITZERLAND

Cardinal Richelieu
From 1624–42 Cardinal Richelieu ran the government of Louis XIII. He crushed the Huguenots and built up French military strength against Spain.

Catalonia
In 1640 the French supported a revolt in Catalonia against Spanish rule. The region came under the protection of Louis XIII until the revolt was crushed in the 1650s.

Catalonia

Portugal in revolt
Spain took over Portugal by force in 1580. Sixty years later the Portuguese rose in revolt and, with help from the French, won back their independence.

PORTUGAL

Douro

LISBON

Tagus

MADRID

SPAIN

Escorial Palace
The vast Escorial Palace outside Madrid was built for Philip II in 1563–84. He ruled his vast European and American empire from here.

Ebro

Guadalquivir

Sardinia

Mediterranean Sea

0		500 km
0		250 miles

STOCKHOLM

SWEDEN

Swedish trade
After 1561
Sweden controlled
much of the coast
with its wealthy trade
in timber, amber
and other goods.

COPENHAGEN

• Memel

PRUSSIA

• Königsberg

Danzig •

Baltic Sea

Stralsund •
• Lübeck

Magdeburg
The sacking of Magdeburg
by Catholic forces in 1631
led to savage acts of
retaliation across Germany.

Brandenburg
• Magdeburg

Oder

Germany **Saxony**
Breitenfeld •
Lützen •

Elbe

Bohemia

Prague •

POLAND

**HOLY ROMAN
EMPIRE**

Danube

Austria

• Nordlingen

VIENNA ■

Spanish intervention
Spanish troops from
Italy regularly fought
French and Protestant
forces in Germany
during the Thirty
Years' War.

HUNGARY

Thrown out!
The Thirty Years' War
began in 1618, when Bohemian
Protestants threw two Austrian
imperial officials out of a
window at Prague Castle.

Dual crown
The Habsburg rulers of Austria
also ran the Holy Roman Empire,
and were in charge of the
imperial forces against France,
Sweden and the Protestants.

**OTTOMAN
EMPIRE**

ROME ■

Adriatic Sea

NAPLES ■ **Naples**

Tyrrhenian Sea

*Ionian
Sea*

The Spanish Mediterranean
Throughout this period,
Naples, Sicily and Sardinia
were part of Spain, despite
French-inspired revolts against
Spanish troops in 1647.

Sicily

The Dutch revolt

As converts to Calvinism, the Dutch came into
conflict with their Spanish Catholic rulers. In 1568
they revolted and declared their independence as
the United Provinces in 1581. Supported by the
French and English, they fought with Spain until
a 12-year truce was declared in 1609. Spain finally
recognized their independence in 1648. An
example of Dutch prosperity can be seen in this
grand area of Amsterdam (above), developed by
wealthy Dutch merchants in the 17th century.

The Thirty Years' War

In 1618 Protestants in Bohemia rose up against
their Catholic Austrian rulers. Protestant and
Catholic states across Germany soon joined in the
fighting. After 1625, the war became more about
territorial power than religion, as Denmark and
then Sweden joined the war on the Protestant side
to expand their power in the Baltic. This painting
(above) shows the king of Sweden leading a
cavalry charge at the Battle of Lützen in 1632.

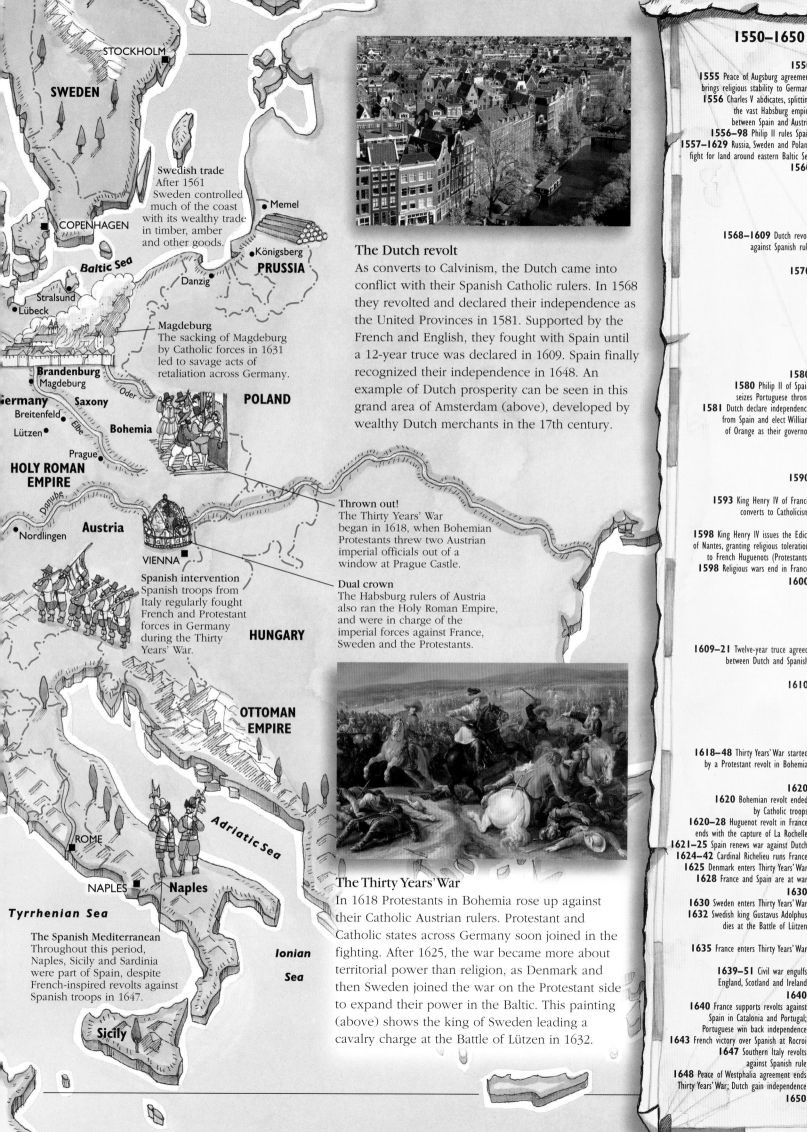

1550–1650

1550
1555 Peace of Augsburg agreement
brings religious stability to Germany
1556 Charles V abdicates, splitting
the vast Habsburg empire
between Spain and Austria
1556–98 Philip II rules Spain
1557–1629 Russia, Sweden and Poland
fight for land around eastern Baltic Sea
1560

1568–1609 Dutch revolt
against Spanish rule
1570

1580
1580 Philip II of Spain
seizes Portuguese throne
1581 Dutch declare independence
from Spain and elect William
of Orange as their governor

1590
1593 King Henry IV of France
converts to Catholicism

1598 King Henry IV issues the Edict
of Nantes, granting religious toleration
to French Huguenots (Protestants)
1598 Religious wars end in France
1600

1609–21 Twelve-year truce agreed
between Dutch and Spanish

1610

1618–48 Thirty Years' War started
by a Protestant revolt in Bohemia

1620
1620 Bohemian revolt ended
by Catholic troops
1620–28 Huguenot revolt in France
ends with the capture of La Rochelle
1621–25 Spain renews war against Dutch
1624–42 Cardinal Richelieu runs France
1625 Denmark enters Thirty Years' War
1628 France and Spain are at war
1630
1630 Sweden enters Thirty Years' War
1632 Swedish king Gustavus Adolphus
dies at the Battle of Lützen

1635 France enters Thirty Years' War

1639–51 Civil war engulfs
England, Scotland and Ireland
1640
1640 France supports revolts against
Spain in Catalonia and Portugal;
Portuguese win back independence
1643 French victory over Spanish at Rocroi
1647 Southern Italy revolts
against Spanish rule
1648 Peace of Westphalia agreement ends
Thirty Years' War; Dutch gain independence
1650

The expansion of Russia

Over the course of 300 years, the small, poor, landlocked state of Muscovy expanded to become, as Russia, one of the major nations in Europe. To do this, it had to overcome huge problems – a small population, vast distances between towns, a terrible climate, and large areas of empty land in which hostile armies could easily hide. The main driving force behind Russian success was Peter the Great, who modelled Russia on the western countries of Europe and almost single-handedly modernized his backward nation. Victories over Sweden, by 1721, gave Russia access to the Baltic Sea, paving the way for future Russian success and territorial gains during the 1700s.

The Urals
The Ural mountains form the border between Europe and Asia. During the late 1500s, the Russians crossed these mountains and built many new towns in Siberia.

polar bear roaming the Arctic tundra

Metal working
Many new state-owned iron and copper works were built in the Urals to exploit the great mineral wealth of the mountains.

Close shave
To make his country more like those in the west, Peter the Great ordered all his lords and nobles to shave off their beards and dress in western fashions.

Building St Petersburg
In 1703 work began on a new capital city, which gave access to the Baltic Sea.

Moscow
After the fall of Constantinople to the Muslim Ottomans in 1453, Moscow became the centre of Orthodox Christianity in Europe.

International trade
Russian merchants traded silk, tea and gems from China, and textiles from Persia and central Asia. Sugar, tobacco and wine were imported from Europe.

Russian navy
Peter the Great studied ship building in England, returning home in 1698 to create a great navy.

Fur trading
During the 1600s, to develop the local fur trade, a series of fortified trading stations were built along the main trade route to China.

serfs (peasants) working on a farm

Controlling the Caspian
In 1723 Russian troops occupied the west and south coasts of the Caspian Sea, but the Persians forced them to give up these areas in 1732.

SWEDEN

Karelia

Ingria

Estonia

Livonia

Ural Mountains

RUSSIA

Siberia

ST PETERSBURG
Narva
Novgorod
Pskov
Moscow
Smolensk
Kazan

Tobolsk
Tomsk
Yeniseysk
Krasnoyarsk
Irkutsk
Kyakht

POLAND

Baltic Sea

Kiev
Poltava
Dnieper
Don

Astrakhan
Azov

KHANATE OF CRIMEA

Sevastopol
Black Sea
Constantinople

Caucasus Mountains

Caspian Sea

OTTOMAN EMPIRE

SAFAVID EMPIRE

The city of Peter the Great

Peter the Great wanted to give Russia "a window on the west", so that it could trade ideas, goods and technology with western Europe. In 1703, he ordered the construction of a new city – St Petersburg – on marshland next to the Neva river at the eastern end of the Baltic Sea. Many thousands of workers died building the city, which includes the Winter Palace (left) and other grand buildings. St Petersburg became the national capital of Russia in 1712 and one of the leading cultural and diplomatic cities in Europe.

Arctic Ocean

Fur trapping
Siberian tribesmen hunted bears and other animals for their meat and fur. They traded these goods with Russian merchants in return for guns and other items.

tree felling for timber

Bering Strait

Alaska

Crossing to America
Russian traders crossed the Bering Strait into Alaska, and in 1784 they established the first Russian settlement there. Alaska was sold to the USA in 1867.

Amur
Amur

CHINA

Pacific Ocean

dotted line shows the extent of Russian territory in 1783

Fortifying the border
In 1650 Russian troops occupied the Amur region, north of China, and built forts along the Amur river border. The region was returned to China in 1689.

0   **500 km**

0   **250 miles**

1450–1800

1450

1478 Led by Ivan III, 'the Great', Muscovy conquers its main rival, Novgorod
1480 Muscovy becomes independent of Mongol Tatar rule

1500
1501 Ivan III expands his territory westwards, towards Poland

1533–84 Reign of Ivan IV, 'the Terrible'

1547 Ivan IV is crowned the first tsar (emperor) of Russia

1550
1552 Russia begins to conquer Tatar khanates north of the Caspian Sea

1581 Russia begins to expand over the Ural mountains and into Siberia
1582 Poland and Sweden prevent Russia from gaining access to the Baltic Sea

1600
1613–45 Reign of Mikhail I, the first tsar of the Romanov family

1637 Russian explorers reach the Pacific coast of Siberia for the first time

1650
1650–89 Russian occupation of the Amur region, north of China

1682–1725 Reign of Peter I, 'the Great'

1696 Russia captures Azov from the Ottomans, giving it access to the Black Sea
1697–98 Peter I travels around western Europe, studying new ideas on how to modernize his country
1700
1700–21 Great Northern War with Sweden brings Russia land around the Baltic Sea
1703 Construction of St Petersburg begins

1712 National capital moved from Moscow to St Petersburg

1750
1762–92 Reign of Catherine II, 'the Great'
1768–74 War against the Ottomans brings gains around the Black Sea
1772 First Partition of Poland: Russia, Austria and Prussia seize Polish territory; Russian frontier extends westwards
1783 Russia captures Crimea
1784 Russians establish first settlement in Alaska
1800

China and Japan

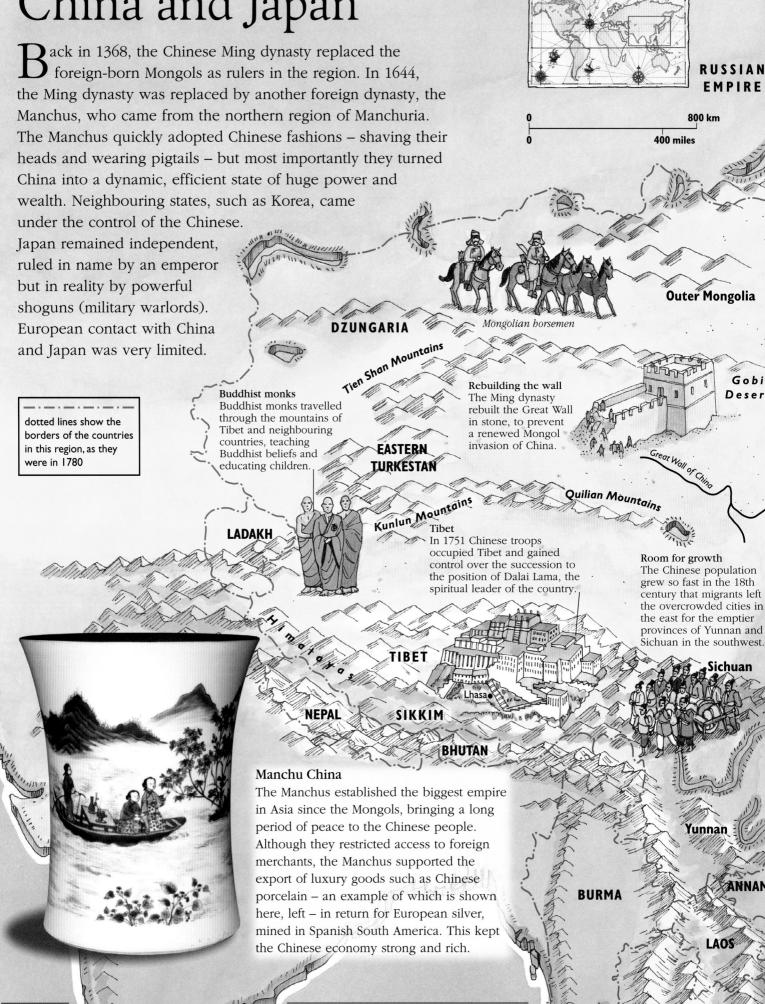

Back in 1368, the Chinese Ming dynasty replaced the foreign-born Mongols as rulers in the region. In 1644, the Ming dynasty was replaced by another foreign dynasty, the Manchus, who came from the northern region of Manchuria. The Manchus quickly adopted Chinese fashions – shaving their heads and wearing pigtails – but most importantly they turned China into a dynamic, efficient state of huge power and wealth. Neighbouring states, such as Korea, came under the control of the Chinese. Japan remained independent, ruled in name by an emperor but in reality by powerful shoguns (military warlords). European contact with China and Japan was very limited.

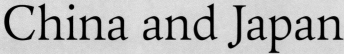

RUSSIAN EMPIRE

0   800 km
0   400 miles

dotted lines show the borders of the countries in this region, as they were in 1780

Mongolian horsemen

Outer Mongolia

DZUNGARIA

Tien Shan Mountains

Gobi Desert

Rebuilding the wall
The Ming dynasty rebuilt the Great Wall in stone, to prevent a renewed Mongol invasion of China.

Great Wall of China

Buddhist monks
Buddhist monks travelled through the mountains of Tibet and neighbouring countries, teaching Buddhist beliefs and educating children.

EASTERN TURKESTAN

Quilian Mountains

Kunlun Mountains

LADAKH

Tibet
In 1751 Chinese troops occupied Tibet and gained control over the succession to the position of Dalai Lama, the spiritual leader of the country.

Room for growth
The Chinese population grew so fast in the 18th century that migrants left the overcrowded cities in the east for the emptier provinces of Yunnan and Sichuan in the southwest.

Himalayas

TIBET

Lhasa

Sichuan

NEPAL   **SIKKIM**

BHUTAN

Yunnan

Manchu China
The Manchus established the biggest empire in Asia since the Mongols, bringing a long period of peace to the Chinese people. Although they restricted access to foreign merchants, the Manchus supported the export of luxury goods such as Chinese porcelain – an example of which is shown here, left – in return for European silver, mined in Spanish South America. This kept the Chinese economy strong and rich.

BURMA

ANNAM

LAOS

28

Forts for furs
In 1689 the Russians swapped a fort in Manchuria for better access to Chinese markets, creating a huge demand for Siberian furs in Beijing.

AMUR

Manchu by name
The name 'Manchu' is thought to come from *Manjusri*, a Buddhist *bodhisattva* (holy man) who lived at Mount Wutai, near Beijing.

Manchuria

Noh drama
Local daimyo (lords) were great supporters of Japanese arts, such as noh drama, the tea ceremony, poetry and painting.

Growing cotton
Cotton fields planted by the Mongols in northern China supplied a booming textile industry in the Yangtze delta to the south.

The Willow Palisade
The Ming built a continuous wooden wall, with gate towers, to protect Chinese settlements north of the Great Wall.

Sea of Japan

Japanese soldier with a Portuguese-style musket

Inner Mongolia

Great Wall of China

■ BEIJING

boat on Grand Canal

pirate ships

JAPAN

● Edo

The Five Highways

● Pyongyang

KOREA

● Azuchi

Kyoto ●

Azuchi castle
The castle of Azuchi, begun in 1576, was designed to dominate the fertile plains. It was an administrative centre as well as a fortress.

Horse post
The Ming set up a courier service to carry messages across the empire. It took seven weeks to travel from north to south China.

Grand Canal

● Pusan

HIRADO

Nagasaki

Ming porcelain

Invading Korea
A Japanese army of 200,000 troops invaded Korea in 1592, but it was driven out by a vast Chinese army and naval force.

Nagasaki
In 1570 the local daimyo (lord) Omura developed the small fishing village of Nagasaki as Japan's main port for foreign trade.

CHINA

Yangtze

● Nanjing

textile production

East China Sea

The Dutch
Dutch merchants set up a fortified trading base on Taiwan in 1622, so that they could trade with mainland China. The island itself did not become part of China until 1683.

In demand
Raw cotton was shipped in along the Grand Canal and down the Yangtze river to supply the major cotton factories of the delta region.

Taiwan

European trade
The Portuguese set up a permanent trading base at Macao in 1557, the first foreign involvement in the Chinese economy.

Guangzhou (Canton) ●

Macao ●

South China Sea

Overseas trade
The Chinese traded cotton textiles, silk, tea, porcelain and ironware with countries throughout southeast Asia and the eastern Indian Ocean in return for European silver.

1500–1800

1500
1500 Chinese population at about 90 million people

1520–21 Portuguese make first direct European trade contact with China
1520s Wako pirates from Japan begin to raid the Chinese coastline

1542 Portuguese first arrive in Japan
1542, 50 Mongols invade Ming China

1548–61 Portuguese convert some Japanese to Christianity
1550
1556 Worst-ever Chinese earthquake kills 850,000 people
1557 Portuguese set up a trading base at Macao
1568 Nobunaga, leader of Oda clan, begins to unify central Japan
1570 Nagasaki developed as main Japanese port for foreign trade
1580 Chinese population now 130 million
1580s Ming empire declines
1582 Hideyoshi succeeds Nobunaga and soon controls eastern and northern Japan
1592, 97 Japan invades Korea
1600
1603 New Tokugawa dynasty of shoguns (military commanders) rules Japan
1609 Dutch set up base in Japan
1615 Nurhachi is Manchu leader
1622 Dutch establish trading base on Taiwan
1627 Revolts break out across China

1637 Manchus govern Korea
1638 37,000 Japanese Christians massacred
1641 Portuguese expelled from Japan
1644 Manchus occupy China; beginning of the Qing dynasty
1650
1650 Chinese population drops to 100 million

1662–1722 Kangxi emperor rules China

1683 Chinese conquer Taiwan
1689 Russians leave Amur region in exchange for trade allowances

1700

1715 Japanese limit trade with Dutch

1727 Chinese agree a frontier with Russia

1736–95 Qianlong emperor rules China

1750
1751 Chinese occupy Tibet
1755–60 Chinese conquer Turkestan and Dzungaria in the far west
1760s Widespread peasant uprisings against Tokugawa government in Japan

1800 Chinese population now at 300 million
1800

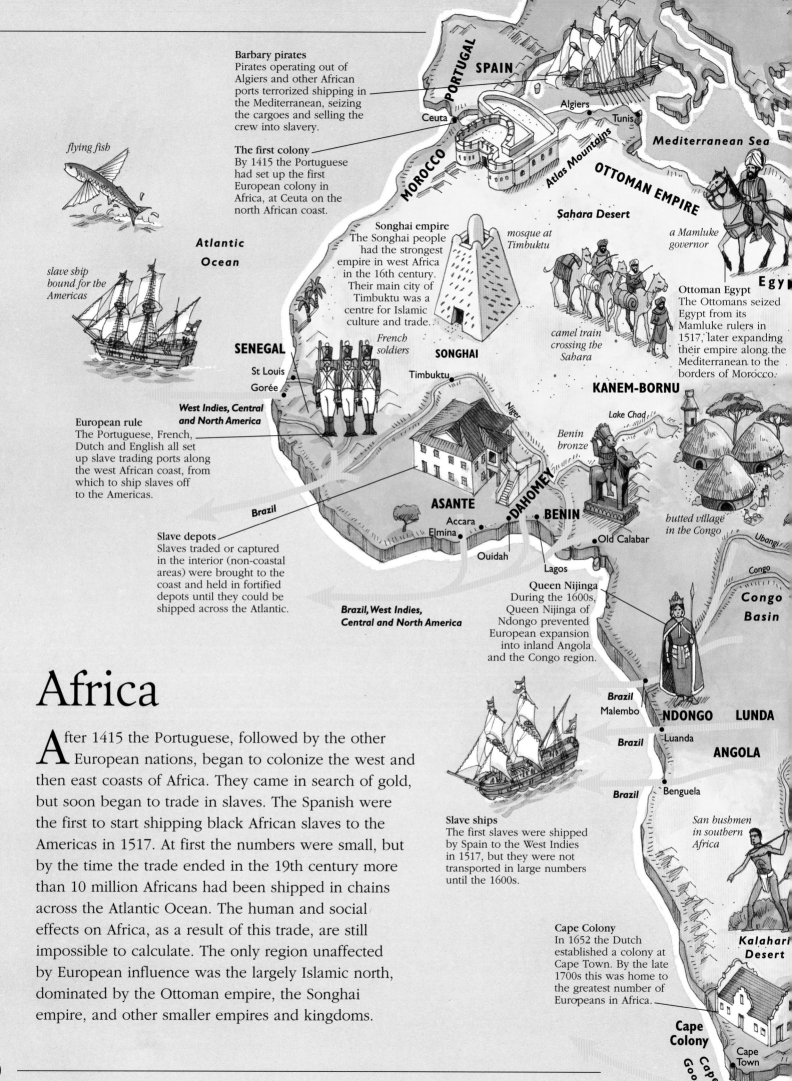

Barbary pirates
Pirates operating out of Algiers and other African ports terrorized shipping in the Mediterranean, seizing the cargoes and selling the crew into slavery.

The first colony
By 1415 the Portuguese had set up the first European colony in Africa, at Ceuta on the north African coast.

flying fish

Atlantic Ocean

slave ship bound for the Americas

Songhai empire
The Songhai people had the strongest empire in west Africa in the 16th century. Their main city of Timbuktu was a centre for Islamic culture and trade.

mosque at Timbuktu

a Mamluke governor

Ottoman Egypt
The Ottomans seized Egypt from its Mamluke rulers in 1517, later expanding their empire along the Mediterranean to the borders of Morocco.

camel train crossing the Sahara

French soldiers

West Indies, Central and North America

European rule
The Portuguese, French, Dutch and English all set up slave trading ports along the west African coast, from which to ship slaves off to the Americas.

Brazil

Slave depots
Slaves traded or captured in the interior (non-coastal areas) were brought to the coast and held in fortified depots until they could be shipped across the Atlantic.

Brazil, West Indies, Central and North America

Benin bronze

hutted village in the Congo

Queen Nijinga
During the 1600s, Queen Nijinga of Ndongo prevented European expansion into inland Angola and the Congo region.

Brazil

Brazil

Brazil

Slave ships
The first slaves were shipped by Spain to the West Indies in 1517, but they were not transported in large numbers until the 1600s.

San bushmen in southern Africa

Cape Colony
In 1652 the Dutch established a colony at Cape Town. By the late 1700s this was home to the greatest number of Europeans in Africa.

Map labels: PORTUGAL, SPAIN, Algiers, Tunis, Ceuta, Mediterranean Sea, MOROCCO, Atlas Mountains, OTTOMAN EMPIRE, Sahara Desert, Egy, SENEGAL, St Louis, Gorée, SONGHAI, Timbuktu, KANEM-BORNU, Lake Chad, Niger, ASANTE, Accara, Elmina, DAHOMEY, BENIN, Ouidah, Lagos, Old Calabar, Congo Basin, Ubangi, Congo, NDONGO, LUNDA, Malembo, Luanda, ANGOLA, Benguela, Kalahari Desert, Cape Colony, Cape Town, Cape of Good Hope

Africa

After 1415 the Portuguese, followed by the other European nations, began to colonize the west and then east coasts of Africa. They came in search of gold, but soon began to trade in slaves. The Spanish were the first to start shipping black African slaves to the Americas in 1517. At first the numbers were small, but by the time the trade ended in the 19th century more than 10 million Africans had been shipped in chains across the Atlantic Ocean. The human and social effects on Africa, as a result of this trade, are still impossible to calculate. The only region unaffected by European influence was the largely Islamic north, dominated by the Ottoman empire, the Songhai empire, and other smaller empires and kingdoms.

The Portuguese east coast

In 1498 the Portuguese navigator Vasco da Gama sailed around the Cape of Good Hope on his way to India. This opened up a new trade route between Europe and India across the Indian Ocean. The Portuguese soon set up a string of trading bases up the east coast, such as at Kilwa (left). These bases stretched from Delagoa Bay in the south to the island of Socotra, at the mouth of the Red Sea, in the north.

Jesuit conversions
Jesuit missionaries arrived in Ethiopia in 1557 to convert the Ethiopians from the Coptic Church to the Roman Catholic Church.

Arab traders
Arab dhows (sailing boats) traded goods with India, the Arabian Peninsula and the Persian Gulf, often in competition and conflict with their Portuguese rivals.

Christians united
The Portuguese sent an army to help their fellow Christian Ethiopians defeat an invading Adali army at Waina Dega in 1543.

Portuguese trade
After 1505 the Portuguese set up a string of trading bases along the east African coast. From here they traded gold, ivory and spices across the Indian Ocean.

Gold
The Shona and Makua people mined and panned for gold near Lake Malawi. They traded it for guns, textiles and other goods with Arab and Portuguese merchants on the coast.

these arrows show the direction and destinations of the slave ships that sailed across the Atlantic from African ports

Cairo
Nile
Arabian Peninsula
India
Arabian Sea
Socotra
Waina Dega
ETHIOPIA
ADAL
Lake Turkana
Rift Valley
Mogadishu
SULTANATE OF ZANZIBAR
Indian Ocean
Lake Victoria
Malindi
Mombasa
Rift
Zanzibar
Kilwa
Lake Tanganyika
Great Mosque at Kilwa
Lake Malawi
Valley
Mozambique
Zambezi
Madagascar
MWENEMUTAPA
Limpopo
Delagoa Bay
Brazil

0
0
2000 km
1000 miles

1482 Portuguese establish a fortress at Elmina in west Africa to protect gold trade
1488 Portuguese navigator Bartolomeu Dias becomes first European to sail around Africa into the Indian Ocean
1498 Vasco da Gama opens up a sea route from Europe, around Africa, to India

1500

1505 Portuguese begin to colonize Mozambique and the rest of the east African coast
1517 Spanish begin shipping slaves to the West Indies
1517 Ottomans conquer Egypt
1527–43 Islamic Adal kingdom attacks Ethiopia
1529 Songhai empire is at its greatest extent

1550

1557 Jesuit missionaries arrive in Ethiopia
1570 King Idris III Aloma creates a powerful Islamic state in Kanem-Bornu
1575 Portuguese begin to colonize Angola

1591 Moroccan force overthrows the Songhai empire
1592 British first ship slaves to the Americas
1598 Portuguese colonize Mombasa

1600

1600 East African kingdom of Mwenemutapa is at its greatest extent

1624–43 Queen Nijinga rules Ndongo
1626 French begin to colonize Senegal and Madagascar
1626–32 Roman Catholicism becomes the official religion of Ethiopia
1637 Dutch capture Elmina from the Portuguese

1650

1652 Omanis from the Arabian Peninsula attack Zanzibar, the first major threat to Portuguese trade in east Africa
1652 Dutch establish Cape Town

1698 Omanis set up the Sultanate of Zanzibar and expel the Portuguese from the east coast

1700

1700 Kingdoms of Asante and Dahomey dominate the west African coast
1705–14 North Africa becomes semi-independent from the Ottoman empire
1713 Britain gains 30-year control over the shipping of African slaves to Spanish America
1724 Dahomey provides slaves for European slave-traders

1750

1750s Powerful Lunda empire emerges in central Africa

1758–83 British and French fight for control of Senegal

1800

The slave trade:
The terrible trade in humans

Slavery has existed throughout human history, but in the 16th century a new and terrible chapter in this story began. In 1502 a Portuguese ship transported west African slaves to the Americas. Regular shipments then started up in 1517. At first this trade was slow, but the increasing demand for labour on the new sugar plantations, and in the mines, outgrew the supply of native Americans. So Africans were brought across the Atlantic to fill the gap. The trade flourished during the 17th and 18th centuries, with approximately 10 million Africans enslaved before the trade ended in the 19th century. The human cost of slavery was huge, and while it brought great wealth to European traders and American landowners, it devastated Africa.

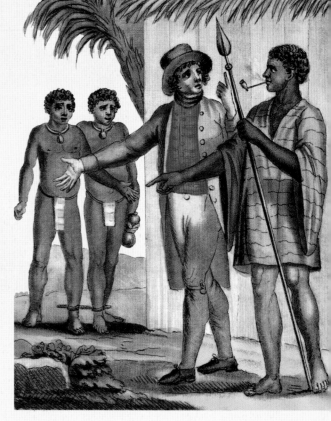

Trading in lives
Slaves captured during warfare between rival African kingdoms, or enslaved by their own leaders, were taken to the coast and sold to European slavers. The picture above shows a man buying slaves at Gorée, a French island off Senegal on the west African coast. Here the slaves were branded (marked with hot irons) and imprisoned in slave depots until a ship arrived to take them to the Americas.

On the plantation
Life on the plantations, such as this sugar plantation in Antigua in the West Indies, was harsh. Slaves were the property of the plantation owner and had no rights of their own. They worked long hours, often from sunrise to sunset, and were often whipped to make them work harder. They did not earn any money, but were given enough food to keep them alive.

Male and female slaves hoe the land in a line, making it ready for planting sugar cane

Overseer makes sure slaves work hard for their master

Even young slave children are forced to work on the land

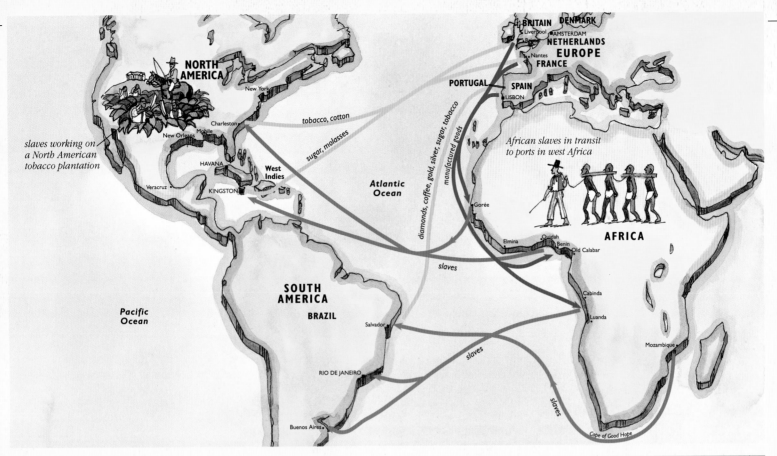

NORTH AMERICA

New York

slaves working on a North American tobacco plantation

Charleston

New Orleans Mobile

HAVANA

Veracruz

KINGSTON

West Indies

tobacco, cotton

sugar, molasses

Atlantic Ocean

Pacific Ocean

SOUTH AMERICA

BRAZIL

Salvador

RIO DE JANEIRO

Buenos Aires

slaves

slaves

slaves

BRITAIN DENMARK

Liverpool AMSTERDAM

NETHERLANDS EUROPE

Nantes FRANCE

PORTUGAL SPAIN

LISBON

diamonds, coffee, gold, silver, sugar, tobacco

manufactured goods

African slaves in transit to ports in west Africa

Gorée

Elmina Ouidah

Benin Old Calabar

AFRICA

Cabinda

Luanda

Mozambique

slaves

Cape of Good Hope

The slave trade triangle

As shown in this map (above), the path of slave ships formed a triangular pattern across the Atlantic Ocean. Ships carrying manufactured goods such as guns and cotton cloth sailed from western European ports to the west African coast. Here the cargo was traded for slaves, who were then shipped across to Brazil, the West Indies, Central and North America. The slaves were sold to the plantation owners and the ships returned home with a rich cargo of sugar, rum, tobacco, cotton, coffee, and sometimes silver and precious stones.

KEY TO MAP: THE 'TRIANGULAR TRADE'

Ships carry manufactured goods from Europe to Africa ⟶
The Middle Passage: slaves are taken across the Atlantic ⟶
Ships return home with raw materials from the Americas ⟶

Remembering the past

Slavery ended during the 19th century, but its impact is still with us today. The economy and social structure of much of Africa has never recovered from the removal of so many young men and women as slaves, while the free descendants of slaves, particularly in the USA, still face unfair treatment and discrimination. This statue (right) is a memorial to those who were slaves on Barbados, a British island in the West Indies.

The Middle Passage

The voyage across the Atlantic Ocean from Africa to the Americas – known as the Middle Passage – took up to 16 weeks. Conditions on board were appalling. Hundreds of slaves were packed tightly into the hold, as this painting shows (above). They were all chained together to stop them from jumping overboard. As many as four out of every ten slaves died during the journey across.

Colonizing North America

When Europeans first arrived in North America, the land puzzled them. The early explorers thought it was Asia and did not realize it was a continent in its own right, while Spanish conquistadors (conquerors) expected to discover gold-filled cities just as they had found earlier in Mexico and Peru. None of them realized just how big or potentially rich and fertile this continent was. Yet slowly Europeans began to colonize this new world, the French and English trapping and trading furs in the north, while farmers from all nations settled in colonies along the east coast. Once the barrier of the Appalachian mountains was crossed in 1671, the way was clear for pioneer settlers to exploit this fertile land to the full.

Henry Hudson
In 1611 Hudson went in search of the Northwest Passage to the Pacific Ocean, but his crew staged a mutiny. Hudson, his young son and seven loyal sailors were left to die in a small boat.

Lake Winnipeg

Canada

Hudson's Bay Company
After 1670, the English Hudson's Bay Company set up bases around Hudson Bay, to trade furs with the native Cree people. The French captured all the bases in 1686.

The Great Lakes

Lake Superior

Rocky Mountains

buffalo grazing

Hunting buffalo
The Plains Indians hunted herds of buffalo for their meat, skins and bones.

tents of the Plains Indians

Mississippi

New Mexico
The Spaniards set up a permanent base at Santa Fe in 1609, but their settlement in the region was limited by the harsh climate.

New Mexico

• Santa Fe

The first settlers

The first European settlers, such as those shown in this painting, inhabited the eastern coastline of North America – the Spaniards in the south, the English, Dutch and Swedes in the centre and the French in the north and along the St Lawrence river. Many of the settlers had fled religious or political persecution in Europe and sought to create a new life in a new world. They survived by growing their own crops and raising livestock, and by trading with the local native Americans. They also received some supplies by ship from Europe.

Spanish pueblo village in the southwest

In search of gold
From 1539–43 the Spaniard Hernando de Soto led an expedition up the Mississippi in search of gold, inflicting great cruelty on the native Americans he met on his way.

Down river
In 1682 Robert de la Salle became the first person to canoe down the Mississippi river. He was disappointed to find it ended up in the Gulf of Mexico, not the Pacific Ocean.

Louisiana

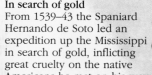

Spanish explorers
In the 1500s, Spain mounted huge military expeditions from Mexico and the Caribbean into North America in search of gold, and to convert the natives to Christianity. They did not succeed.

Mexico

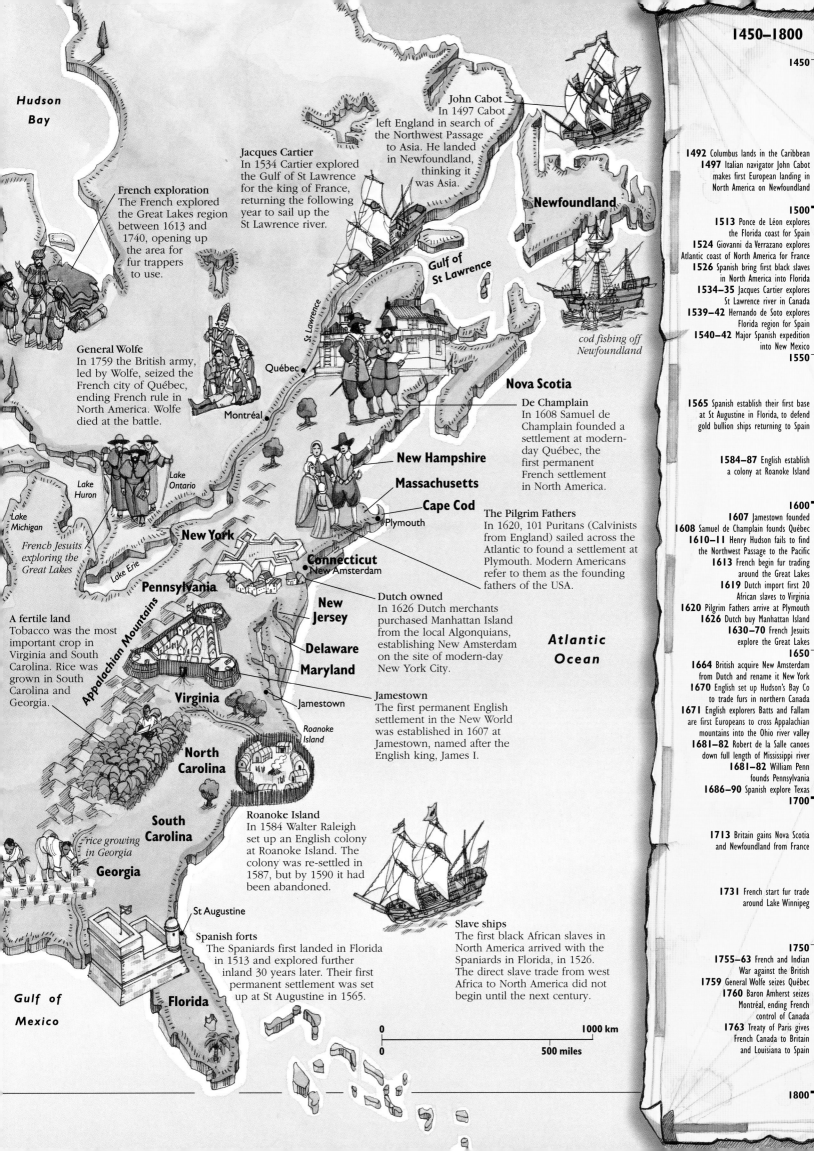

Hudson Bay

John Cabot
In 1497 Cabot left England in search of the Northwest Passage to Asia. He landed in Newfoundland, thinking it was Asia.

Jacques Cartier
In 1534 Cartier explored the Gulf of St Lawrence for the king of France, returning the following year to sail up the St Lawrence river.

Newfoundland

Gulf of St Lawrence

cod fishing off Newfoundland

French exploration
The French explored the Great Lakes region between 1613 and 1740, opening up the area for fur trappers to use.

General Wolfe
In 1759 the British army, led by Wolfe, seized the French city of Québec, ending French rule in North America. Wolfe died at the battle.

St Lawrence

Québec

Montréal

Nova Scotia

De Champlain
In 1608 Samuel de Champlain founded a settlement at modern-day Québec, the first permanent French settlement in North America.

New Hampshire

Massachusetts

Cape Cod

Plymouth

Lake Huron

Lake Michigan

Lake Ontario

Lake Erie

French Jesuits exploring the Great Lakes

New York

Pennsylvania

The Pilgrim Fathers
In 1620, 101 Puritans (Calvinists from England) sailed across the Atlantic to found a settlement at Plymouth. Modern Americans refer to them as the founding fathers of the USA.

Connecticut
New Amsterdam

New Jersey

Delaware

Maryland

Dutch owned
In 1626 Dutch merchants purchased Manhattan Island from the local Algonquians, establishing New Amsterdam on the site of modern-day New York City.

Atlantic Ocean

A fertile land
Tobacco was the most important crop in Virginia and South Carolina. Rice was grown in South Carolina and Georgia.

Appalachian Mountains

Virginia

Jamestown

Jamestown
The first permanent English settlement in the New World was established in 1607 at Jamestown, named after the English king, James I.

Roanoke Island

North Carolina

South Carolina

rice growing in Georgia

Georgia

Roanoke Island
In 1584 Walter Raleigh set up an English colony at Roanoke Island. The colony was re-settled in 1587, but by 1590 it had been abandoned.

St Augustine

Spanish forts
The Spaniards first landed in Florida in 1513 and explored further inland 30 years later. Their first permanent settlement was set up at St Augustine in 1565.

Slave ships
The first black African slaves in North America arrived with the Spaniards in Florida, in 1526. The direct slave trade from west Africa to North America did not begin until the next century.

Gulf of Mexico

Florida

0 ___ 1000 km
0 ___ 500 miles

1450

1492 Columbus lands in the Caribbean
1497 Italian navigator John Cabot makes first European landing in North America on Newfoundland

1500

1513 Ponce de Léon explores the Florida coast for Spain
1524 Giovanni da Verrazano explores Atlantic coast of North America for France
1526 Spanish bring first black slaves in North America into Florida
1534–35 Jacques Cartier explores St Lawrence river in Canada
1539–42 Hernando de Soto explores Florida region for Spain
1540–42 Major Spanish expedition into New Mexico

1550

1565 Spanish establish their first base at St Augustine in Florida, to defend gold bullion ships returning to Spain

1584–87 English establish a colony at Roanoke Island

1600

1607 Jamestown founded
1608 Samuel de Champlain founds Québec
1610–11 Henry Hudson fails to find the Northwest Passage to the Pacific
1613 French begin fur trading around the Great Lakes
1619 Dutch import first 20 African slaves to Virginia
1620 Pilgrim Fathers arrive at Plymouth
1626 Dutch buy Manhattan Island
1630–70 French Jesuits explore the Great Lakes

1650

1664 British acquire New Amsterdam from Dutch and rename it New York
1670 English set up Hudson's Bay Co to trade furs in northern Canada
1671 English explorers Batts and Fallam are first Europeans to cross Appalachian mountains into the Ohio river valley
1681–82 Robert de la Salle canoes down full length of Mississippi river
1681–82 William Penn founds Pennsylvania
1686–90 Spanish explore Texas

1700

1713 Britain gains Nova Scotia and Newfoundland from France

1731 French start fur trade around Lake Winnipeg

1750

1755–63 French and Indian War against the British
1759 General Wolfe seizes Québec
1760 Baron Amherst seizes Montréal, ending French control of Canada
1763 Treaty of Paris gives French Canada to Britain and Louisiana to Spain

1800

The age of absolutism

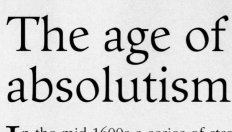

In the mid-1600s a series of strong monarchs emerged in Europe. They held total control and believed in 'absolutism', the idea that the power of the state was embodied in the king, who was answerable to nobody. The greatest of these monarchs was Louis XIV of France, who famously said, "L'état, c'est moi" ("I am the state"). Under Louis, France fought a series of wars against the Habsburgs of Spain and Austria to become the most powerful state in Europe by 1715. To the east, Prussia began to emerge as the strongest state in Germany, while Austria fought off its many enemies to become the leading state in central Europe by 1750.

0 ———————————————— 500 km
0 ———————————————— 250 miles

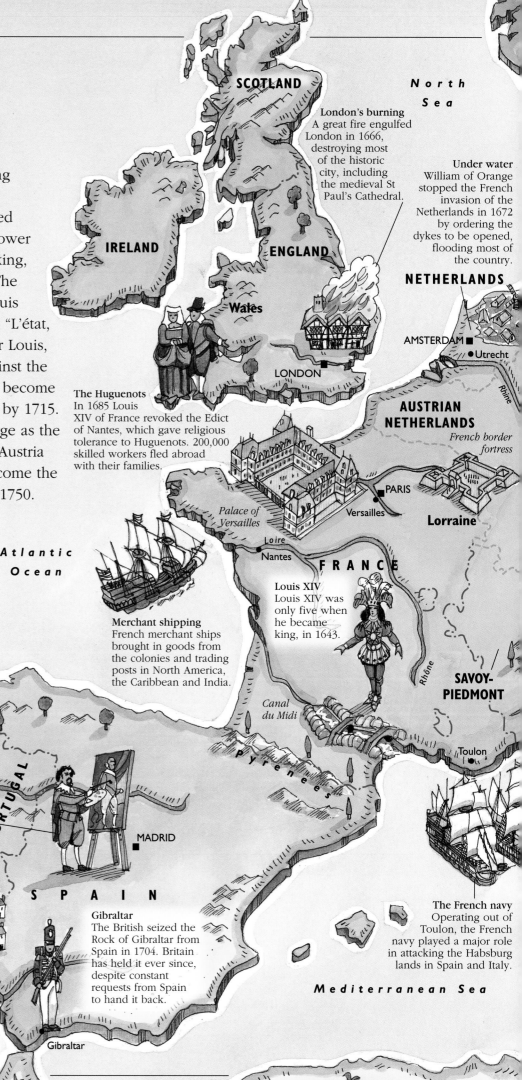

London's burning
A great fire engulfed London in 1666, destroying most of the historic city, including the medieval St Paul's Cathedral.

Under water
William of Orange stopped the French invasion of the Netherlands in 1672 by ordering the dykes to be opened, flooding most of the country.

French border fortress

The Huguenots
In 1685 Louis XIV of France revoked the Edict of Nantes, which gave religious tolerance to Huguenots. 200,000 skilled workers fled abroad with their families.

Atlantic Ocean

Merchant shipping
French merchant ships brought in goods from the colonies and trading posts in North America, the Caribbean and India.

Louis XIV
Louis XIV was only five when he became king, in 1643.

Spanish art
Spanish power declined during the 1600s, but the country enjoyed a golden age of painting and architecture, with artists such as Velázquez and Zurbarán much in demand for their life-like portraits and still-life works.

Tidal wave
In 1755 a massive earthquake caused a tidal wave to engulf the Portuguese capital, Lisbon, killing thousands of people.

Gibraltar
The British seized the Rock of Gibraltar from Spain in 1704. Britain has held it ever since, despite constant requests from Spain to hand it back.

The French navy
Operating out of Toulon, the French navy played a major role in attacking the Habsburg lands in Spain and Italy.

Mediterranean Sea

SCOTLAND
North Sea
IRELAND
ENGLAND
Wales
LONDON
NETHERLANDS
AMSTERDAM
Utrecht
AUSTRIAN NETHERLANDS
Rhine
PARIS
Versailles
Palace of Versailles
Loire
Nantes
FRANCE
Lorraine
Rhône
SAVOY-PIEDMONT
Canal du Midi
Pyrenees
Toulon
PORTUGAL
MADRID
LISBON
SPAIN
Gibraltar

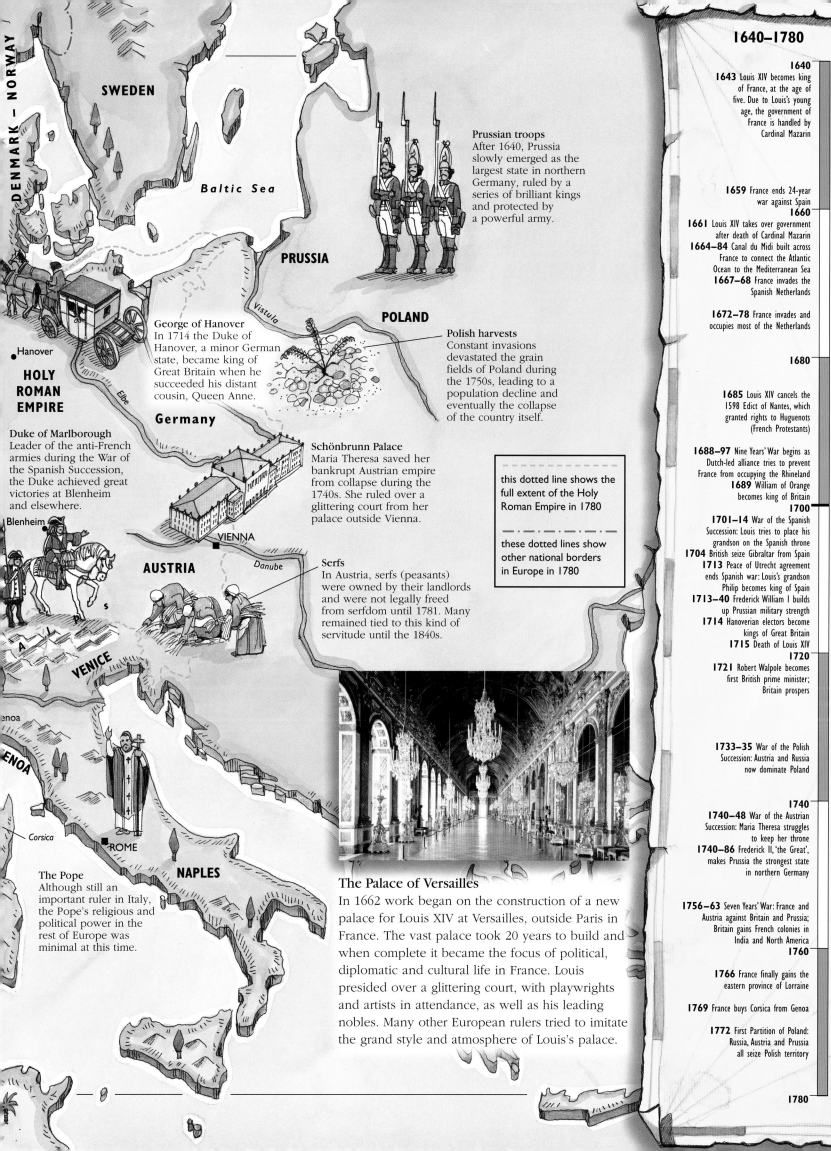

SWEDEN

DENMARK – NORWAY

Baltic Sea

PRUSSIA

Prussian troops
After 1640, Prussia slowly emerged as the largest state in northern Germany, ruled by a series of brilliant kings and protected by a powerful army.

Vistula

POLAND

George of Hanover
In 1714 the Duke of Hanover, a minor German state, became king of Great Britain when he succeeded his distant cousin, Queen Anne.

Polish harvests
Constant invasions devastated the grain fields of Poland during the 1750s, leading to a population decline and eventually the collapse of the country itself.

• Hanover

HOLY ROMAN EMPIRE

Elbe

Germany

Duke of Marlborough
Leader of the anti-French armies during the War of the Spanish Succession, the Duke achieved great victories at Blenheim and elsewhere.

Blenheim

Schönbrunn Palace
Maria Theresa saved her bankrupt Austrian empire from collapse during the 1740s. She ruled over a glittering court from her palace outside Vienna.

this dotted line shows the full extent of the Holy Roman Empire in 1780

these dotted lines show other national borders in Europe in 1780

VIENNA

AUSTRIA

Danube

Serfs
In Austria, serfs (peasants) were owned by their landlords and were not legally freed from serfdom until 1781. Many remained tied to this kind of servitude until the 1840s.

A l p s

VENICE

enoa

ENOA

Corsica

The Pope
Although still an important ruler in Italy, the Pope's religious and political power in the rest of Europe was minimal at this time.

ROME

NAPLES

The Palace of Versailles

In 1662 work began on the construction of a new palace for Louis XIV at Versailles, outside Paris in France. The vast palace took 20 years to build and when complete it became the focus of political, diplomatic and cultural life in France. Louis presided over a glittering court, with playwrights and artists in attendance, as well as his leading nobles. Many other European rulers tried to imitate the grand style and atmosphere of Louis's palace.

1640

1643 Louis XIV becomes king of France, at the age of five. Due to Louis's young age, the government of France is handled by Cardinal Mazarin

1659 France ends 24-year war against Spain

1660

1661 Louis XIV takes over government after death of Cardinal Mazarin

1664–84 Canal du Midi built across France to connect the Atlantic Ocean to the Mediterranean Sea

1667–68 France invades the Spanish Netherlands

1672–78 France invades and occupies most of the Netherlands

1680

1685 Louis XIV cancels the 1598 Edict of Nantes, which granted rights to Huguenots (French Protestants)

1688–97 Nine Years' War begins as Dutch-led alliance tries to prevent France from occupying the Rhineland

1689 William of Orange becomes king of Britain

1700

1701–14 War of the Spanish Succession: Louis tries to place his grandson on the Spanish throne

1704 British seize Gibraltar from Spain

1713 Peace of Utrecht agreement ends Spanish war: Louis's grandson Philip becomes king of Spain

1713–40 Frederick William I builds up Prussian military strength

1714 Hanoverian electors become kings of Great Britain

1715 Death of Louis XIV

1720

1721 Robert Walpole becomes first British prime minister; Britain prospers

1733–35 War of the Polish Succession: Austria and Russia now dominate Poland

1740

1740–48 War of the Austrian Succession: Maria Theresa struggles to keep her throne

1740–86 Frederick II, 'the Great', makes Prussia the strongest state in northern Germany

1756–63 Seven Years' War: France and Austria against Britain and Prussia; Britain gains French colonies in India and North America

1760

1766 France finally gains the eastern province of Lorraine

1769 France buys Corsica from Genoa

1772 First Partition of Poland: Russia, Austria and Prussia all seize Polish territory

1780

The intellectual revolution:
An enlightened view of the world

During the mid-17th century a new way of looking at the world began to flourish in Europe. This movement is known as the Enlightenment, as it was a time of new ideas based on human logic and reason rather than the old religious beliefs of the Christian Church. The Enlightenment had a huge impact not just on philosophy and politics but also on science and invention. The Enlightenment movement was opposed by the Catholic Church, but some rulers supported these new ideas, setting up universities and scientific societies, and granting religious and political freedoms to their subjects.

Politics
The Enlightenment changed political thinking and influenced the French Revolution of 1789. In 1791–92 the English pamphlet-writer Thomas Paine (1737–1809, right) wrote *The Rights of Man*, in support of the revolution, but was forced to flee to France. There he wrote *The Age of Reason* (1795), attacking Christianity, and was almost executed by guillotine.

Philosophy
The French philosopher René Descartes (1596–1650, left) is often seen as the founder of modern philosophy, putting logic and reason at the heart of his thinking. He summed up his beliefs in the phrase, "I think, therefore I am." A century later, Voltaire (1694–1778) wrote a stream of witty pamphlets, novels and plays that were read by people all across Europe, making the new ideas of the Enlightenment very popular.

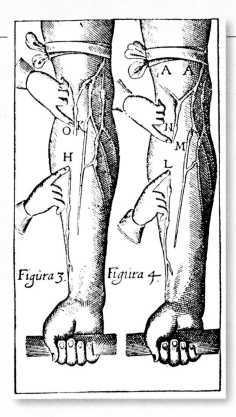

Physics

The English scientist Isaac Newton (1642–1727, right) demonstrated that white light is made up of a spectrum of colours. He did this by 'refracting' it through a glass prism. Most important of all, he defined the three laws of motion and the universal law of gravitation – the invisible force of attraction between objects.

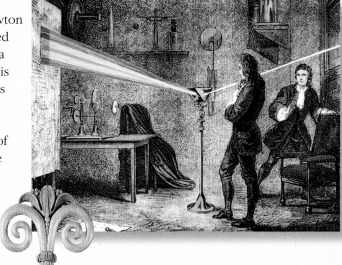

Anatomy

In 1628 William Harvey published *De Motu Cordis* – 'On the Motion of the Heart' – in which he suggested that blood is pumped by the heart, and that it is constantly circulating around the body. His explanations overturned medical beliefs that had been followed since the Greeks, 1,400 years before.

Eyepiece lens turns image right way up

Lenses magnify subject about 21 times, which allowed Galileo to see only one-third of the Moon at one time

Object lens magnifies subject but turns it upside down

Astronomy

Both Galileo Galilei (1564–1642) and Johannes Kepler (1571–1630) developed the basic ideas of Copernicus (see page 14). Galileo invented a telescope for studying the movement of the planets. Kepler discovered that the planets move around the Sun in ellipses (ovals) rather than circles, and move fastest when they are closest to the Sun.

Galileo used this telescope to view the heavens in 1609. The telescope gives a restricted view, as the lenses are small.

Microscopy

Robert Hooke (1635–1703) developed a powerful 'compound' or multi-lens microscope (left) for studying very small organisms. He was the first person to use the word 'cell' to describe the tiny units out of which all living things are made.

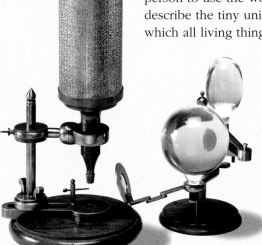

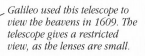

Ornamental stand for the telescope

Exploring the Pacific

The first Europeans entered the Pacific Ocean in the 1500s, looking for a new sea route to Asia and its riches. In the 1600s merchants came in search of spices, setting up trading posts throughout the East Indies (Indonesia). Many islands in the Pacific remained unknown to Europeans, as did Australia, which Dutch navigators either mistook for New Guinea or sailed right around. It was not until 1770 that Captain Cook made a proper landing there. Eighteen years later, 750 British convicts became the first permanent European settlers in Australia.

KEY TO VOYAGES

Ferdinand Magellan		1519–21
Alvaro de Mendaña		1567–69
Abel Tasman		1642–43
James Cook: 1st voyage		1768–71

CHINA

Macao

tin mining

Malay Peninsula

Malacca

pepper

EAST INDIES

Sumatra

Indian Ocean

BATAVIA

Java

Solor

coffee

Kupang

Timor

Silk trade
Portuguese merchants based in Macao supplied fine Chinese silk to the Spanish in the Philippines.

PHILIPPINES

Manila

South China Sea

gold ore

Spanish Catholic church

aborigines in Borneo

Ternate

Moluccas Islands

Amboina

Banda Islands

cloves

Guam

Polynesians fishing

New Guinea

sugar

nutmeg

Tasman trading with natives

Crossing the Pacific
Magellan took four months to cross the Pacific. He landed in Guam and then eventually reached the Philippines, where he was killed in a skirmish with local people.

Pacific trade
Spanish galleons regularly crossed the Pacific, taking silver from Acapulco in Mexico and returning from Manila in the Philippines with Chinese silk.

Cannibals
Mendaña sent some of his crew ashore in the Solomon Islands to find fresh water. They were attacked by cannibals.

SOLOMON ISLANDS

Reefed
Captain Cook ran his ship *Endeavour* aground on the Barrier Reef. He and his crew had to stop to repair the large hole in the ship's hull.

FIJI

TONGA

Batavia
Batavia was the HQ of the Dutch East Indies Company, a trading organization that dominated the spice trade in the region.

Malacca
The Portuguese built a large fort at Malacca, so that they could dominate the sea route between the Indian Ocean and the South China Sea.

AUSTRALIA

Aborigines
About 300,000 Aborigines lived in Australia before the Europeans arrived. Their numbers dropped after foreign settlement began, due to the diseases and violence brought by the settlers.

Great Barrier Reef

Botany Bay
The first 750 British convicts landed in Botany Bay in 1788 to serve their prison sentences in Australia. 160,000 more followed until this practice was stopped in 1868.

Botany Bay

a ship from Abel Tasman's fleet

Tasmania

North Island

South Island

NEW ZEALAND

Tasmania
Tasman sent a carpenter ashore to plant a flag on what he called Van Diemen's Land, named after the governor-general of Dutch Batavia. The island is now called Tasmania, after Tasman himself.

Brutal welcome
When Captain Cook landed on the North Island of New Zealand, he and his crew were attacked by the native Maori people. In the skirmish, several Maoris were shot.

The spice trade

Spices such as nutmeg, cloves and peppers were much prized in Europe for seasoning food. Until the 1500s, spices reached Europe only via the Arab trading networks of the Indian Ocean and Middle East and were very expensive. In 1519 Magellan set out to reach the Spice Islands (the Moluccas) by sailing west from Spain – but it was the Portuguese and later the Dutch who gained control of this rich trade with Europe. This painting (left) shows the Dutch trading base at Batavia in the East Indies.

Men overboard
Álvaro de Mendaña and his crew suffered from hunger and scurvy, a disease caused by a lack of the Vitamin C found in fresh fruit and vegetables. When crew members died, their bodies were thrown overboard.

Hawaii

Pacific Ocean

Marquesas Islands

Tahiti

Álvaro de Mendaña's ship, San Jeronimo

three ships from Ferdinand Magellan's fleet

Cook's first voyage
In 1768–71 Captain Cook completed his first voyage. He and his crew sailed all the way around New Zealand and then discovered Australia.

Captain Cook's ship, Endeavour

temple at Chichén Itzá

MEXICO

● *Acapulco*

parrot

llama

Amazon rainforest

Callao ■ **LIMA**

Inca city of Machu Picchu

0   2000 km

0   1000 miles

1500–1800

1500

1511 Portuguese seize Malacca and Malay Peninsula

1520–21 Ferdinand Magellan crosses the Pacific, the first European to do so

1567–69 Álvaro de Mendaña explores the South Pacific and discovers the Solomon Islands
1571 Spanish found Manila as the capital of the Philippines
1579 Francis Drake crosses the Pacific from California, in North America, to the Philippines

1595–96 Álvaro de Mendaña dies in an attempt to set up a Spanish colony in the Solomons
1596 First arrival of the Dutch in Java

1600

1602 Dutch East Indies Co is founded
1605–06 Dutch navigator Willem Jantszoon explores the north coast of Australia but thinks it is part of New Guinea
1606–07 Luis de Torres sails around New Guinea, proving it is an island

1619 Dutch seize Batavia and set up Dutch East Indies Co headquarters there
1623 Dutch drive British out of the Spice Islands (Moluccas)
1629 Dutch drive Portuguese out of the Spice Islands

1641 Dutch seize Malacca from the Portuguese
1642–43 Abel Tasman discovers Van Diemen's Land (Tasmania), New Zealand, Fiji and Tonga

1667 Dutch complete their conquest of the Spice Islands

1684 Dutch seize most of Java and eastern Sumatra

1700

1700 Dutch dominate European trade with the East Indies (Indonesia)

1768–71 Cook's first voyage: he circumnavigates (sails around) New Zealand and discovers Australia
1772–75 Cook's second voyage: he explores Antarctica
1776–79 Cook's third voyage: he sails north, to find an inlet into the Arctic Ocean, and discovers Hawaii, where he dies

1788 First British convicts land in Botany Bay, Australia
1792 First British settlement in New Zealand

1800

The American Revolution

In 1775 13 of the British colonies in North America rose up in revolt. They protested against British attempts to restrict their freedom and to tax them without giving them any representation in parliament. Led by George Washington, and later supported by the French, the colonists declared their independence in 1776 and won a series of military victories before the war ended in 1783. This victory gave birth to a new nation, the United States of America, which at first stretched only as far inland as the Mississippi river. Eventually, it extended right across the continent to the Pacific Ocean in the west.

George Washington

George Washington (1732–99) was a colonial farmer in Virginia who fought for the British against the French in the 1750s. He was the ideal person to command the American forces against the British and led them to victory in 1781. As the first president of the newly independent United States, from 1789–97, he led the nation with great skill and determination.

Loyalists
Americans from New York and South Carolina, loyal to the British crown, fled north to Canada along with Mohawks who had fought for the British. They settled in Ontario and the provinces near to the sea.

Paul Revere
On 18 April 1775, silversmith Paul Revere rode through the night to warn people that British troops were coming to capture military stores at Concord.

Saratoga
A British attempt to isolate the New England colonies from the rest of America was defeated at Saratoga in 1777.

The Boston Tea Party
Colonists upset by the British government's tax on imported tea dumped a cargo of tea into Boston harbour in 1773.

Legend of Betsy Ross
Betsy Ross was asked to make the first American flag using six-pointed stars, but said that five-pointed stars 'would look better'.

Crossing the Delaware
On Christmas Day 1776, George Washington led his recently defeated army across the icy Delaware river, surprising the British and winning a crucial battle at Trenton.

A new capital
In 1791 the decision was taken to build a new national capital on the Potomac river. It was named 'Washington' in honour of the first president, George Washington.

CANADA

UNITED STATES OF AMERICA

Ontario

Québec

Montréal

Lake Superior

Lake Michigan

Lake Huron

Lake Erie

Lake Ontario

Mississippi

New Hampshire

Concord
Bunker Hill
Lexington
Boston

Massachusetts

Rhode Island

Connecticut

Hudson

New York

Saratoga

New York

Princeton
Trenton

Pennsylvania

Philadelphia

Brandywine

Baltimore

Delaware

New Jersey

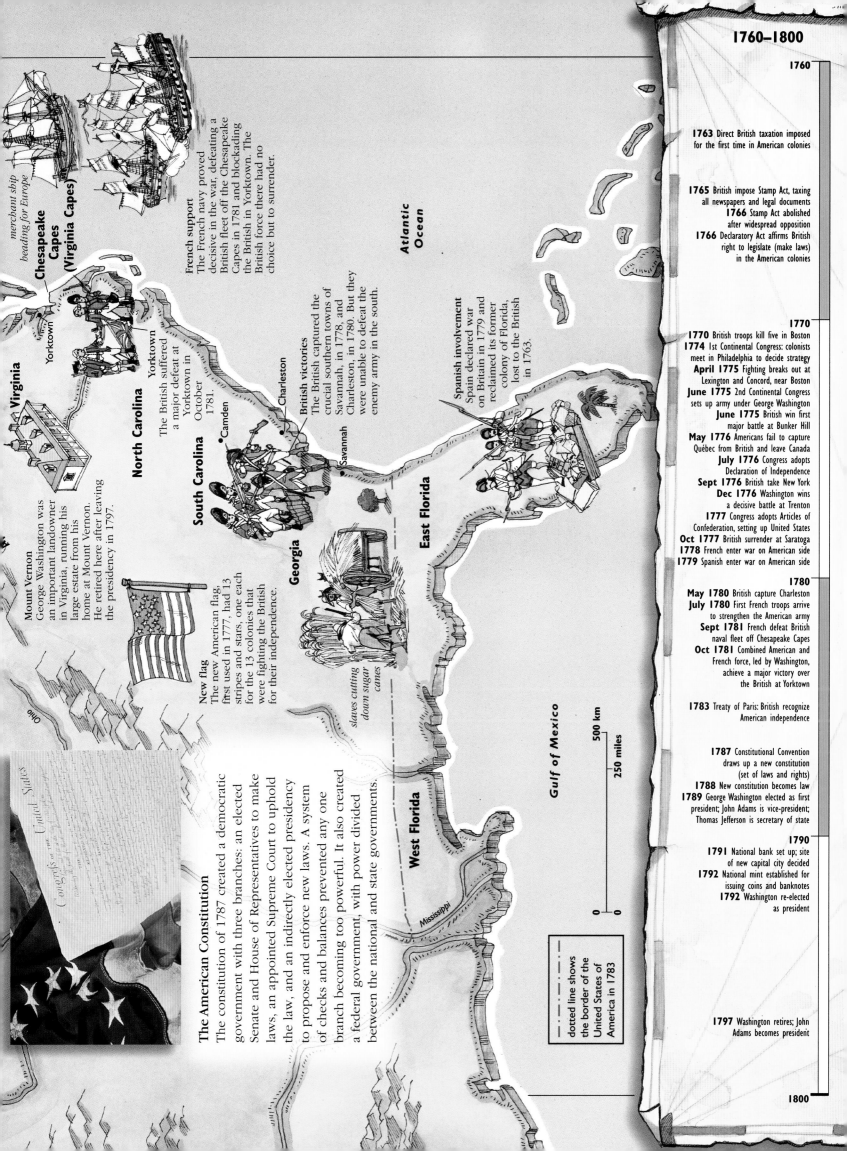

merchant ship heading for Europe

Chesapeake Capes (Virginia Capes)

French support
The French navy proved decisive in the war, defeating a British fleet off the Chesapeake Capes in 1781 and blockading the British in Yorktown. The British force there had no choice but to surrender.

Virginia

Yorktown

North Carolina

Yorktown
The British suffered a major defeat at Yorktown in October 1781.

Camden

Charleston

South Carolina

British victories
The British captured the crucial southern towns of Savannah, in 1778, and Charleston, in 1780. But they were unable to defeat the enemy army in the south.

Savannah

Georgia

East Florida

Spanish involvement
Spain declared war on Britain in 1779 and reclaimed its former colony of Florida, lost to the British in 1763.

Atlantic Ocean

Mount Vernon
George Washington was an important landowner in Virginia, running his large estate from his home at Mount Vernon. He retired here after leaving the presidency in 1797.

Ohio

New flag
The new American flag, first used in 1777, had 13 stripes and stars, one each for the 13 colonies that were fighting the British for their independence.

slaves cutting down sugar canes

West Florida

Gulf of Mexico

Mississippi

500 km

250 miles

0

0

The American Constitution
The constitution of 1787 created a democratic government with three branches: an elected Senate and House of Representatives to make laws, an appointed Supreme Court to uphold the law, and an indirectly elected presidency to propose and enforce new laws. A system of checks and balances prevented any one branch becoming too powerful. It also created a federal government, with power divided between the national and state governments.

United States

Congress of the United States

dotted line shows the border of the United States of America in 1783

1760

1763 Direct British taxation imposed for the first time in American colonies

1765 British impose Stamp Act, taxing all newspapers and legal documents
1766 Stamp Act abolished after widespread opposition
1766 Declaratory Act affirms British right to legislate (make laws) in the American colonies

1770

1770 British troops kill five in Boston
1774 1st Continental Congress: colonists meet in Philadelphia to decide strategy
April 1775 Fighting breaks out at Lexington and Concord, near Boston
June 1775 2nd Continental Congress sets up army under George Washington
June 1775 British win first major battle at Bunker Hill
May 1776 Americans fail to capture Québec from British and leave Canada
July 1776 Congress adopts Declaration of Independence
Sept 1776 British take New York
Dec 1776 Washington wins a decisive battle at Trenton
1777 Congress adopts Articles of Confederation, setting up United States
Oct 1777 British surrender at Saratoga
1778 French enter war on American side
1779 Spanish enter war on American side

1780

May 1780 British capture Charleston
July 1780 First French troops arrive to strengthen the American army
Sept 1781 French defeat British naval fleet off Chesapeake Capes
Oct 1781 Combined American and French force, led by Washington, achieve a major victory over the British at Yorktown

1783 Treaty of Paris: British recognize American independence

1787 Constitutional Convention draws up a new constitution (set of laws and rights)
1788 New constitution becomes law
1789 George Washington elected as first president; John Adams is vice-president; Thomas Jefferson is secretary of state

1790

1791 National bank set up; site of new capital city decided
1792 National mint established for issuing coins and banknotes
1792 Washington re-elected as president

1797 Washington retires; John Adams becomes president

1800

The French Revolution

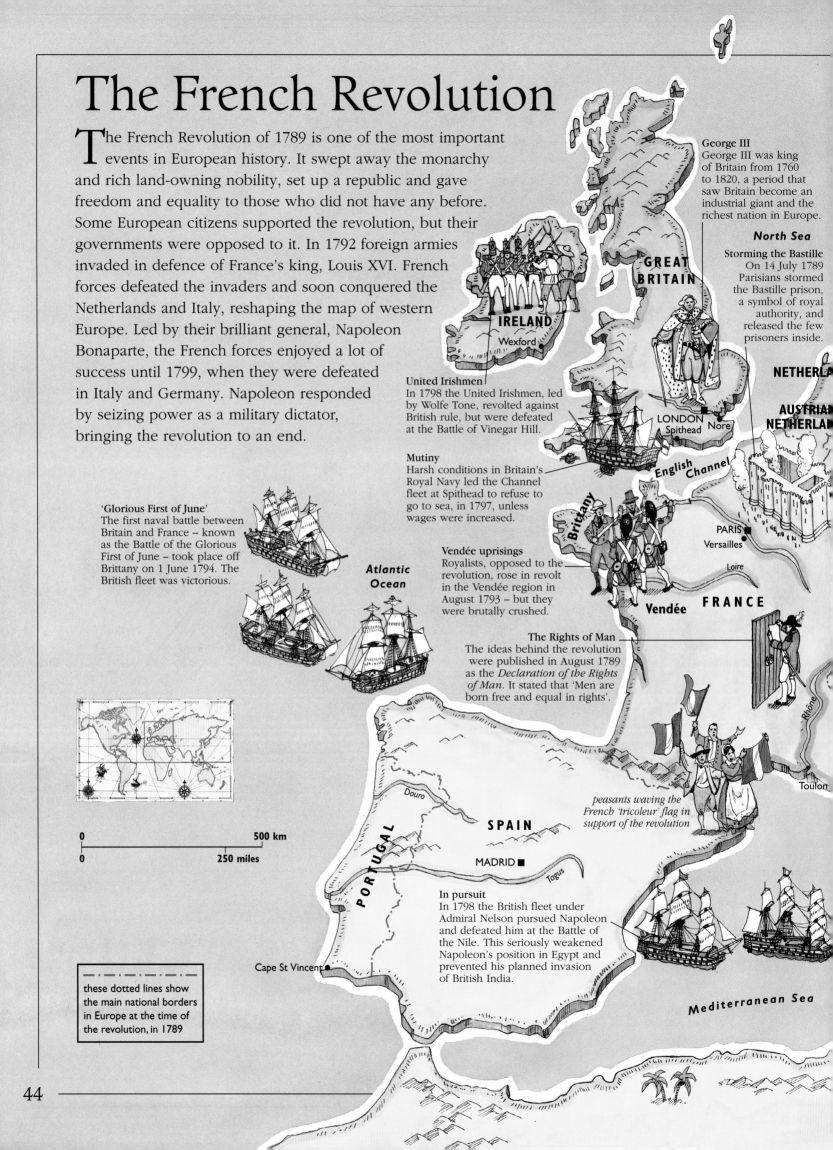

The French Revolution of 1789 is one of the most important events in European history. It swept away the monarchy and rich land-owning nobility, set up a republic and gave freedom and equality to those who did not have any before. Some European citizens supported the revolution, but their governments were opposed to it. In 1792 foreign armies invaded in defence of France's king, Louis XVI. French forces defeated the invaders and soon conquered the Netherlands and Italy, reshaping the map of western Europe. Led by their brilliant general, Napoleon Bonaparte, the French forces enjoyed a lot of success until 1799, when they were defeated in Italy and Germany. Napoleon responded by seizing power as a military dictator, bringing the revolution to an end.

George III
George III was king of Britain from 1760 to 1820, a period that saw Britain become an industrial giant and the richest nation in Europe.

North Sea

Storming the Bastille
On 14 July 1789 Parisians stormed the Bastille prison, a symbol of royal authority, and released the few prisoners inside.

GREAT BRITAIN

IRELAND

Wexford

NETHERLA

AUSTRIAN NETHERLAN

United Irishmen
In 1798 the United Irishmen, led by Wolfe Tone, revolted against British rule, but were defeated at the Battle of Vinegar Hill.

LONDON
Spithead   Nore

English Channel

Mutiny
Harsh conditions in Britain's Royal Navy led the Channel fleet at Spithead to refuse to go to sea, in 1797, unless wages were increased.

PARIS
Versailles

Loire

Brittany

'Glorious First of June'
The first naval battle between Britain and France – known as the Battle of the Glorious First of June – took place off Brittany on 1 June 1794. The British fleet was victorious.

Atlantic Ocean

Vendée uprisings
Royalists, opposed to the revolution, rose in revolt in the Vendée region in August 1793 – but they were brutally crushed.

Vendée   FRANCE

The Rights of Man
The ideas behind the revolution were published in August 1789 as the *Declaration of the Rights of Man*. It stated that 'Men are born free and equal in rights'.

Rhône

Toulon

peasants waving the French 'tricoleur' flag in support of the revolution

Douro

SPAIN

PORTUGAL

MADRID

Tagus

In pursuit
In 1798 the British fleet under Admiral Nelson pursued Napoleon and defeated him at the Battle of the Nile. This seriously weakened Napoleon's position in Egypt and prevented his planned invasion of British India.

Cape St Vincent

Mediterranean Sea

0   500 km
0   250 miles

these dotted lines show the main national borders in Europe at the time of the revolution, in 1789

44

RUSSIA

Baltic Sea

Prussia
Prussia emerged in the 1700s as the most powerful state in northern Europe. Along with Austria, it declared war on revolutionary France in 1792 to restore the French monarchy.

Partitioning Poland
Three times – in 1772, 1793 and 1795 – Prussia, Russia and Austria divided Poland up between them. The Poles did not regain their independence until 1918.

PRUSSIA

Elbe

BERLIN

Vistula

POLAND

Germany

Rhine

Danube

AUSTRIAN EMPIRE

VIENNA

Marie Antoinette
Marie Antoinette, daughter of the Austrian empress, was married to the French king Louis XVI at the age of 14. She was executed for treason in 1793.

Danube

Commander-in-chief
Napoleon emerged as the leading French commander, thanks to his brilliant campaigns and victories in Italy in 1796–97.

Sava

GENOA

OTTOMAN EMPIRE

Corsica

ROME

Island home
Napoleon Bonaparte was born on 15 August 1769 on the French island of Corsica, which until the previous year had been part of the Italian state of Genoa.

Sardinia

Sicily

MALTA

Beheading the king and queen

Due to the monarchy's rising debts, Louis XVI was forced to summon the Estates-General (parliament) in May 1789 to raise taxes. The ministers of the Third Estate (representing the commoners) were angered by this and soon broke away to form a national assembly. Their demands for political reform led to the revolution, which broke out in July 1789 and reached its peak with Louis's execution in January 1793. The queen of France, Marie Antoinette, was also beheaded in October of the same year (above).

1789
May Estates-General meets but soon collapses
June Third Estate of commoners sets up National Assembly
July Parisians storm the Bastille prison
Aug 'Declaration of the Rights of Man' published
1790

1791

June French king Louis XVI and his queen, Marie Antoinette, try to flee Paris

1792
April France declares war on Austria
July France declares war on Prussia
Sept France abolishes monarchy and becomes a republic
Nov French defeat Austrians and seize the Austrian Netherlands
1793
Jan Louis XVI executed on the guillotine
Jan Second Partition of Poland
Feb–Mar France declares war on Britain and the Dutch republic
Feb First Coalition of European powers formed against France
Mar–Oct Royalist uprising in the Vendée
1794
June 1793–July 1794 Robespierre leads a reign of terror against enemies of the revolution

June British defeat French fleet at the Battle of the Glorious First of June

1795
Jan French conquer the Dutch republic
April France and Prussia make peace

Oct Directory takes power in France
Oct Third Partition of Poland: partition of the country between Austria, Prussia and Russia ends Polish independence
1796
Feb British naval victory over Spain (a French ally) off Cape St Vincent
April Bonaparte commands French forces against Austrians in Italy

1797
April, May British Royal Navy twice mutinies over pay and service conditions

Oct British defeat Dutch fleet at Camperdown off the Dutch coast
Oct Austria and France make peace

1798
June United Irishmen fail to win independence from Britain
July Napoleon defeats Egyptians at the Battle of the Pyramids
Aug Nelson defeats Napoleon at the Battle of the Nile

1799
Mar Austria again declares war on France
Mar, April French forces defeated in Germany and Italy
June Britain, Austria and Russia form the Second Coalition
Nov Napoleon overthrows Directory and sets up a three-man Consulate
1800

Index

This index lists the main peoples, places and topics that you will find in the text in this book. It is not a full index of all the place names and physical features to be found on the maps.

Acknowledgements

The publisher would like to thank the following for permission to reproduce their material. Every care has been taken to trace copyright holders. However, if there have been unintentional omissions or failure to trace copyright holders, we apologize and will, if informed, endeavour to make corrections in any future edition.

Key: *b* = bottom, *c* = centre, *l* = left, *r* = right, *t* = top

Pages 6*cl* Bridgeman Art Library, London/Capitol Collection, Washington; 6–7*b* Corbis/Svenja-Foto Zefa; 6*tr* Bridgeman Art Library/Universitäts Bibliothek, Göttingen; 7*tl* The Art Archive/Culver Pictures; 7*tr* The Art Archive/Gunshots; 9*tl* Bridgeman Art Library/The National Maritime Museum, UK; 11*bl* The Art Archive; 12*tl* Corbis/Gianni Dagli Orti; 13*bl* The Art Archive/Archivo des Indias, Seville; 14*tl* Science & Society Picture Library; 14*cl* Bridgeman Art Library/British Library, London; 14*br* Bridgeman Art Library/Galleria dell'Academia, Florence; 15*tl* Bridgeman Art Library/Museo degli Argenti, Palazzo Pitti, Florence; 17*tr* Bridgeman Art Library/Private Collection; 17*br* Photolibrary/The Travel Library Ltd; 19*tr* The Art Archive/Museum der Stadt Wien/Dagli Orti; 21*b* British Museum; 21*tl* Photolibrary/Jon Arnold Images; 22*tl* The Art Archive; 25*tr* Corbis/Keren Su; 25*br* Bridgeman Art Library/Royal Library, Sweden; 28*bl* Bridgeman Art Library/Private Collection; 31*tl* Corbis/Werner Forman; 32*tr* Bridgeman Art Library/Bibliotheque des Artes Decoratifs, Paris; 32*b* The Art Archive; 33*bl* Corbis/Tony Arruzza; 33*br* The Art Archive; 34*l* Corbis/Burstein Collection; 37*br* Corbis/Massimo Listri; 38*l* The Art Archive/Institut de France, Paris; 38*r* Bridgeman Art Library/British Library; 39*tl* Science Photo Library/Dr Jeremy Burgess; 39*bl* Science & Society Picture Library; 39*tr* Science Photo Library; 39*br* Scala/Museo della Scienze, Florence; 41*tl* Bridgeman Art Library/Rijksmuseum, Amsterdam; 42*tl* Corbis/Christie's Images; 45*r* Corbis/Gianni Dagli Orti.

All illustrations by Mark Bergin